渋かきの
しぶが
そのまま
甘みかな

峻

A Life of Awakening

A Life of Awakening
The Heart of the Shin Buddhist Path

Takamaro Shigaraki

Translated by David Matsumoto

Published by Hōzōkan Publications
Shōmen-dōri Karasuma-higashi iru
Shimogyō-ku, Kyoto, Japan 〒600-8153
Tel. +81-75-343-5656

The frontispiece consists of the
calligraphy and artwork of Takamaro Shigaraki.
The calligraphy is of a poem, which states,
"Shibugaki no shibu ga sono mama amami kana."
This is rendered into English as, "Ah! How very sweet!/
Is the bitterness of the/Bitter persimmon."

Cover design by Arlene Kato
Calligraphy by Reverend Akio Miyaji

Copyright © 2005 by Takamaro Shigaraki
All Rights Reserved

ISBN4-8318-8954-7

Printed in Japan
February 2005
First Edition

Contents

Author's Preface ... xi
Translator's Notes ... xv

Part One The Shin Buddhist Path

Chapter One The Fundamental Principles of Buddhism
  The Teachings of Gautama Buddha ... 3
    Buddha's Final Words
    What Is the Buddha?
    Aim of the Buddhist Teachings
  The Development of Buddhism ... 14
    Buddhism after the Death of Gautama Buddha
    Renunciant Buddhism
    Householder Buddhism
    Formation of the Pure Land Teachings
    Hōnen and the Pure Land Teachings

Chapter Two The Pure Land Buddhist Path
  Amida Buddha ... 23
    Immortalization of Gautama Buddha
    Amida Buddha as Symbol
    Jinen
    Wisdom and Compassion
    Buddha-Body and Buddha-Name
  The Primal Vow of Amida Buddha ... 39
    Truth and Non-truth
    Amida Buddha's Primal Vow
    Buddha's Enlightenment and Our Enlightenment
    Eastern Logic and Western Logic
  The Pure Land Buddhist Path ... 48

Hearing the Name and Seeing the Buddha
Saying the Name and Hearing the Name
Path of Teaching, Practice, and Realization

Chapter Three   The Shin Buddhist Path
  The Path that Shinran Walked   58
    Constant Practice of the *Nembutsu*
    Living the *Nembutsu*
  The *Nembutsu* of "Choice"   65
    The *Nembutsu* Alone Is True and Real
    Nembutsu as "Living"
    Continuous Practice of The *Nembutsu* Every Day
  Nembutsu and *Shinjin*   71
    Nembutsu History
    Psychology of the *Nembutsu*
    Nembutsu and *Shinjin*

Part Two   Shinjin

Chapter One   The Idea of *Shin* in Buddhism
  General Notions of *Shin*   87
  Belief and Faith   88
    Secular Notions of *Shin*: Belief
    General Religious Notions of *Shin*: Faith
  Buddhist Notions of *Shin*   92
    Shin as *Prasāda*
    Shinjin is Non-dualistic and Subjective
    Shinjin as the Experience of Awakening
    Shinjin as Knowing

Chapter Two   *Shinjin* in Shin Buddhism
  Shinjin in Shinran's Thought   98

  Shinjin That is Wisdom
  Shinjin as Awakening
  Shinjin as Becoming
 Traditional Approaches to *Shinjin*   106
  Past Interpretations of *Shinjin*
  Objective Interpretations of *Shinjin*
  Subjective Understandings of *Shinjin*
 The Threefold *Shinjin* of the Primal Vow   114
  Three Minds of the Primal Vow
  Three Aspects of *Shinjin*

Chapter Three Deep Mind, True Mind, and Mind of Aspiration
 Deep Mind   117
  Psychological Perspective
  One Who Is Falling Into Hell
  What Is *Tariki*?
  Conditional Arising and *Tariki*
  Religion as Path
 True Mind   136
  Philosophical Perspective
  Transformation of Life
  To Die and Be Born
 Mind of Aspiration   148
  Ethical Perspective
  Aspiring for Buddhahood To Save Sentient Beings

Part Three Shin Buddhist Life

Chapter One Salvation in Shin Buddhism
 Types of Religious Salvation   157
  Shopenhauer's Theory of Happiness

Three Ways of Seeking Happiness
  Salvation as the Fulfillment of Desire   161
    Supernatural Power
    Petitionary Prayers and Miracles
  Salvation through Self-Control   165
    Will of a Transcendent, Absolute Being
    Faith and Self-Modification
  Salvation as the Establishment of Personal
    Subjectivity   169
    Basic Principles of the World and Human Beings
    Establishment of a New Personal Subjectivity

Chapter Two   *Shinjin* and Human Life
  The Ethics of *Shinjin*   180
    Shinjin and Society
    Ultimate Truth and Worldly Truth
    Living in *Shinjin*
  The Starting Point for Understanding Buddhism   193
    The Basic Commonality of All Life
    The Teaching "Not to Kill"
    The Logic of Harmonious Living
  A True Disciple of the Buddha   205
    Soft and Gentle Heart-Firm and Resolute Mind
    Eyes that See Beyond the Secular World
    A Single, Unhindered Path

Chapter Three   The Shin Buddhist Way of Life
  Living with "Prayers for the World"   215
    Shinran's Instruction
    Amida Buddha's Vows
    Vows for the Adornment of the Buddha's Land

The Wish for Human Fulfillment 223
   True Freedom
   The Process of Human Fulfillment
Aspiring for the Fulfillment of Society 227
   True Equality
   The Process of Societal Fulfillment
Directing Virtue in Our Return to This World 232
   Meaning of Birth in the Pure Land
   Persons who Direct Virtue in Their Return to This World

Author's Preface

In September 1999, I received the opportunity to speak about the fundamental principles of Shin Buddhism during three days of intensive lectures at the Graduate Theological Union in Berkeley, California. Most of those in attendance had some prior connection with Buddhism or Shin Buddhism. However, we were also joined by many persons from various other religious traditions. I was not certain whether my thoughts would be sufficiently conveyed at such a venue. But I was happy to receive favorable comments from the attendees, and was grateful that my own hopes seemed to have been attained. This small volume arose out of my notes for those lectures, with a few minor revisions.

Through the lectures I came to realize that if the teaching of Shin Buddhism is to gain general acceptance in the future, more than anything else, it must be clearly grounded in Eastern logic and particularly in the principles of Mahayana Buddhism.

As long as Shin Buddhism remains stuck as the abstract and sectarian doctrine of the Shin Buddhist religious institutions, it cannot claim to represent an authentic Buddhist teaching. Further, it will not be accepted by the people of the world as a legitimate alternative to Christianity, Islam, or other religions. And, certainly, it will never be studied with sufficient interest by persons in these contemporary times. Therefore, I believe that the traditional doctrine of Shin Buddhism must be re-examined, and in its place a new teaching must be formulated. That new approach must offer an immediate return to the fundamental principles of Mahayana Buddhism, and engage directly the basic intentions of Shinran, the founder of Shin Buddhism. It must also be capable of responding to the many and various problems that the people of the world will come to face in this new century.

My understanding of Shin Buddhism, which I have presented here, has been borne out of this aspiration. I am afraid, however, that my thoughts are truly wanting. For their completion I can only look forward in anticipation to the young scholars who will carry on these efforts after me. I sincerely hope that Shin Buddhist studies of the future will continue to point in this direction and be addressed with even more diligence and thoroughness.

These lectures took place as part of the Yehan Numata Lectures, and I feel profound gratitude for the late Mr. Numata's abiding benevolence in support of academic endeavors. I also wish to thank the Bukkyō Dendō kyōkai for its considerable contribution of founds in support of this publication. In addition, all of the planning and preparation for these lectures was done through the efforts of David Matsumoto of the Institute of Buddhist Studies in Berkeley, California and Professor Mitsuya Dake of the Department of Intercultural Communication of Ryūkoku University in Kyoto, Japan. I would like to express my deep gratitude to them.

The publication of this text has come about through the good offices of President Shichihei Nishimura and Mr. Kenyu Ikeda of Hōzōkan Publications in Kyoto. To them

Author's Preface

I also offer my sincere appreciation.

If this small volume may in some way prove helpful in allowing the teachings of Shin Buddhism and Amida Buddha to spread to the people of Japan and the world, I will be most gratified.

Takamaro Shigaraki
Kyoto, Japan
September 19, 2000

Translator's Notes

With this text, *A Life of Awakening: The Heart of the Shin Buddhist Path,* an important voice rejoins an ongoing discussion in the West concerning Shin Buddhist thought and practice. Takamaro Shigaraki begins this work with the simple declaration that "Shin Buddhism is a path for our attainment of Buddhahood." To many this statement might appear to be an obvious one, requiring no explanation or elaboration. For Dr. Shigaraki, however, it represents an essential focal point, which when carefully examined will allow the heart and value of the Shin Buddhist teaching to become fully realized in a human life.

Shin Buddhism (*Jōdo Shinshū* in Japanese) is a school of Pure Land Buddhism founded by Shinran (1173-1262) in Kamakura-era Japan. In the centuries since its inception, it has become a major school of Buddhism in Japan in terms of the number of its followers, the richness of its tradition, the highly organized structure of its institutions, and its well-developed liturgy and cultural ethos. In the Hongwanji and Ōtani branches sectarian scholarship and contemporary studies of Shin Buddhism operate in parallel with one another. The classic studies of the former branch have been introduced in small part in the West, with much of it reflecting the traditional approaches adopted in orthodox thought.

Over one hundred years ago Shin Buddhism was brought to the West by immigrants from Japan, resulting in a thriving Shin Buddhist community, primarily among people of Japanese ancestry. In recent years the character of Western Shin Buddhism has begun to change as a growing number of non-Japanese practitioners and scholars have come to take an interest in it. Still, when compared to other forms of Buddhism that arrived after it, Shin Buddhism has remained until recent times relatively "under the radar screen" of attention of both the majority population and the scholarly community in the English-speaking world. Yet that has also begun to change as the result of the discussion about Shin Buddhism that is now being carried on in both the academy and the local sangha. Dr. Shigaraki, who has been following this conversation with great interest, now offers to it his own expertise, insights, and aspirations.

According to Shinran *Jōdo Shinshū* is literally the "true essence of the Pure Land way" of enlightenment. It is a path of teaching, practice and realization, which is directed to beings from Amida Buddha so that we may attain birth in the Pure Land. Dr. Shigaraki explores the implications of that path from both theoretical and practical perspectives. He explains that, as a path for our attainment of enlightenment, Shin Buddhism involves many forms of practice. In a broader sense, it also reveals a path of true humanness, a life of awakening in which we are able to encounter true reality in the midst of the emptiness and falsity of our human lives. By thus exploring the nuances and implications of the Shin Buddhist path of enlightenment, Dr. Shigaraki is able to highlight its significance in our individual and social lives today.

The Author

Takamaro Shigaraki is a Buddhist priest and scholar. He was born in 1926, the second son in the family of Reverend Chiyu Shigaraki, the resident priest of Kyōen-ji, a Jōdo Shinshū Buddhist temple in Hiroshima prefecture. As a young man he received the tokudo ordination in the Shin Buddhist Hongwanji branch and then went on to study Buddhism at Ryūkoku University in Kyoto. After completing his undergraduate and graduate studies at that university and at the Shūgaku-in academy of the Hongwanji, he became an instructor at Ryūkoku. He was appointed to the position of professor of Shin Buddhist Studies in 1970 and became the resident priest of Kyōen-ji in 1975.

Dr. Shigaraki's long scholastic career culminated with his being awarded the degree of Doctor of Literature (*bungaku hakase*). He also served as President of Ryūkoku University from 1989 to 1995. Now Professor Emeritus of Shin Buddhist Studies at Ryūkoku, he is also the Chairman of the Bukkyō Dendō Kyōkai (Buddhist Promoting Foundation) in Tokyo, Japan.

Although not widely known outside of the Japanese world of religious studies, Takamaro Shigaraki is in fact one of the leading Shin Buddhist scholars in the world today. While thoroughly grounded in classic Pure Land and Shin Buddhist studies, his perspective differs greatly from the orthodox approaches of Hongwanji sectarian scholarship. For one thing, he believes it crucial that any study of the Shin Buddhist path combine academic rigor with a deep involvement of one's religious heart, mind, and life. Thus, for him the features of the Shin Buddhist path, such as *shinjin*, *nembutsu*, the Primal Vow, or merit transference need to be examined thoroughly, using all of the objective academic tools available. And yet, he maintains, that path can never be understood truly unless, in his words, one walks out onto it "at the risk of one's own subjectivity." For the same reason he is able to view Amida Buddha and the Pure Land not as entity or place, but as dynamic symbols or ideal spheres, which serve as the motives for authentic religious life.

Dr. Shigaraki also feels deeply that in the Western, English-speaking world Shin Buddhism must be examined in a way that differs from the orthodox perspectives to which it has been traditionally bound. He suggests that such an approach needs to be based in Mahayana Buddhist thought or as he calls it, the "logic of the East." Thus, he contrasts Shin Buddhist thought with that of theistic religions, which presume the existence of a transcendent god or a heavenly realm of peaceful reward. In fact, he claims, this kind of dualistic and objective interpretation of Shin Buddhism has created great misunderstanding as to its structure and purport both in Japan and in the West. As a result, its adoption and acceptance by Western Buddhist seekers has been delayed.

His works in Japanese are voluminous, ranging from his scholarly treatments of Pure Land doctrinal developments in India, China, and Japan, to ground-

Translator's Notes

breaking examinations of life science and deeply personal expressions of his encounter with religious reality. His scholarly works include: *Jōdokyō ni okeru shin no kenkyū* [A Study of Shinjin in Pure Land Buddhism] (Kyoto: Nagata Bunshōdō, 1974), *Shinran ni okeru shin no kenkyū* [A Study of Shinjin in Shinran's Thought] (Kyoto: Nagata Bunshōdō, 1990), *Bukkyō no Seimeikan* [Buddhist Life Perspectives] (Kyoto: Hōzōkan, 1994), and *Kyōgyōshō Monrui Kōgi* [Lectures on *Passages Revealing the True, Teaching, and Realization*] (Kyoto: Hōzōkan, 1999).

Dr. Shigaraki has also written a great number of works for the general readership, including *Shinshū Kyōdanron* [Shin Buddhist Institutional Theory] (Kyoto: Nagata Bunshōdō, 1975), *Shinshū Nyūmon* [Introduction to Shin Buddhism] (Kyoto: Hyakkaen, 1977), *Gendai Shinshū Kyōgaku* [Contemporary Shin Buddhist Doctrinal Studies] (Kyoto: Nagata Bunshōdō, 1979), *Anjin Ketsujōshō Kōwa* [Lectures on the *Anjin Ketsujōshō*] (Kyoto: Yobigoesha, 1983), *Shinshū to Gendai Shakai* [Shin Buddhism and Contemporary Society] (Kyoto: Hōzōkan, 1984), *Shinshū no Taii* [The Essence of Shin Buddhism] (Kyoto: Hōzōkan, 2000), and many others.

This Text

The present text developed out of the notes of lectures that Dr. Shigaraki delivered at the Institute of Buddhist Studies in 1999. Those notes were originally published in Japanese as *Shinshū no Taii* [The Essence of Shin

Buddhism] in 2000. The title, *A Life of Awakening: The Heart of the Shin Buddhist Path,* has been chosen for this English translation for a number of reasons. First, it seeks to pay reference and homage to an earlier work that introduced Dr. Shigaraki's thoughts to the English-speaking world more than two decades ago: *The Buddhist World of Awakening* (Honolulu: The Buddhist Study Center of Hawaii, 1982). The present text reflects a development and expansion of many of the themes presented in that earlier work.

Moreover, for Dr. Shigaraki, "awakening" represents the core of the Buddha's enlightenment and Shinran's perspective on *shinjin*. On the one hand, the Buddhist concept of awakening symbolizes the arising of wisdom, where one is able to see things exactly as they are through eyes that transcend the world. In that sense, the idea of awakening can be explored in an objective or descriptive manner. At the same time, awakening could be said to represent the innermost reality of an individual's religious experience, in which one's ego-burdened self is abandoned and one's new self is born. In this sense, awakening represents a declaration of understanding, appreciation, and action by the religious being.

One can clearly see that Dr. Shigaraki's approach to Shin Buddhism is both scholarly and religious ("spiritual" is the word he uses). His work, including this text, therefore finds its place among important contemporary commentaries that combine scholastic rigor and objectivity, with a deeply religious insight borne of subjective practice and experience. Other noteworthy

Translator's Notes

works are: *River of Fire, River of Water: An Introduction to the Pure Land Thought of Shin Buddhism* (New York: Doubleday, 1998) and *Shin Buddhism: Bits of Rubble Turn into Gold* (New York: Doubleday, 2002) by Taitetsu Unno, *The Promise of Boundless Compassion: Shin Buddhism for Today* (Honolulu: Buddhist Study Center Press: 2002) by Alfred Bloom, and *Ocean: An Introduction to Jōdo Shinshū Buddhism* (Berkeley: Wisdom-Ocean Publications, 1997) by Kenneth Tanaka.

The Translation

The author's unique perspective on Shin Buddhist thought necessitates a threefold approach to the translation of his ideas into English.

First, some Sanskrit, Chinese, or Japanese terms have been left untranslated. Dr. Shigaraki takes the position that the rendering of certain terms into English could result in fatal misunderstandings of their underlying meanings. For instance, he feels that translating the term *shinjin* (信心) into English as "faith" or "belief" would reduce a complex idea to a simplistic and dualistic concept. His treatment of the term *tariki* (他力), which is usually translated literally as "Other Power," reflects a similar approach. The author criticizes this rendering, for it makes uni dimensional the otherwise complex notion of "other" in Pure Land Buddhism. Furthermore, he feels, "Other Power" seems to characterize Shin Buddhism as a religion of power, rather than a "religion as path."

Thus, *shinjin*, *tariki*, *nembutsu* (念仏) and some other

terms have not been translated. By explaining the meaning and significance of those terms, he seeks to offer them as new English Buddhist terms, complex in structure and meaning, while bearing a rich history and the potential for elucidating key ideas in Shin Buddhist thought in a new way to a new audience.

In contrast, another set of terms have been translated into English, for it was felt that by doing so the text would be able to benefit from terms rich in religious and theological connotation. Examples include the following: Heart and mind for *kokoro* (心), belief for *shinrai* (信頼), faith for *shinkō* (信仰), prayer for *inori* (いのり), wish or aspiration for *negai* or *gan* (願), and salvation for *kyūsai* (救済) or *sukui* (救い).

In still other cases, the translator has chosen to coin certain terms so as to bring attention to the author's unique perspective on certain elements of the Shin Buddhist path. For instance, the term "de-absolutize" is a rendering of *sōtaika suru* (相対化する). It is intended to refer to the process of negating our tendency to attribute absolute value or substance to concepts that are in fact relative and limited. "Personal subjectivity," is a translation of *shutaisei* (主体性), is meant to point to the deepest level of the self, which must be experienced directly. It is not the product of any conceptualized speculation, nor is it something perceived as the object of dualistic or scientific views. "Harmonious living" is a rendering of the term *kyōsei* (共生). It is intended to overlap in many ways with the concepts of symbiosis or conviviality, but without the biological or social

Translator's Notes

limitations that those terms might possess.

The translator hopes that his choice and usage of these terms will not interfere with the reader's appreciation of the author's intentions. Any confusion that might result herein is solely the fault of the translation and not of the original text.

Acknowledgements

Sincere appreciation is directed to the many people and organizations that made this translation possible. I would first like to thank Dr. Takamaro Shigaraki for entrusting his important thoughts to one who is minimally capable of expressing them in English. I would like to acknowledge the considerable efforts of Professor Mitsuya Dake of Ryūkoku University in support of Dr. Shigaraki's lectures at the Institute of Buddhist Studies and the development of this English text. The generous guidance of Dean Richard Payne, Professor Eisho Nasu and Professor Lisa Grumbach of the Institute of Buddhist Studies was also invaluable. I would like to thank Haru Matsumune and Natalie Fisk for their tireless efforts in the proofing and editing of this text. I wish to acknowledge the encouragement and advice of Mr. Kenyu Ikeda of Hōzōkan Publications of Kyoto, Japan. Finally, I would like to offer heartfelt gratitude to the Yehan Numata Endowment Fund, the Buddhist Churches of America Research and Propagation Program and the George Aratani Endowment for the IBS Center for Contemporary Shin Buddhist Studies, which were the sources of funding for Dr. Shigaraki's lectures and the development of this text.

David Matsumoto
Mountain View, California
December 2003

Part One

The Shin Buddhist Path

The Fundamental Principles of Buddhism

The Teachings of Gautama Buddha

Shin Buddhism is a path for our attainment of Buddhahood. It is a path taught by Shinran (1173-1262 C.E.), but it actually originated with the teaching of Gautama Buddha (463-383 B.C.E.), also known as Sakyamuni Buddha, of ancient India. Even though Shinran lived over fifteen hundred years after the death of Gautama Buddha, his teaching of Shin Buddhism clearly inherited and revealed the essence of the Buddha's teaching, especially as it was directed to lay householders living at the lowest levels of society. For that reason, I would first like to present an outline of the Buddhist path as it developed from the teaching of Gautama Buddha to that of Shinran.

Buddha's Final Words

As he lay dying, Gautama Buddha offered in his final words to his followers a straightforward explanation of the fundamental principles of the Buddhist teachings. These words are preserved in a Pali text, the *Digha-nikāya*, and have also been transmitted in a Chinese scripture, known as the *Last Teaching [of the Buddha] Sutra*, which appears in the *Long Āgama Sutras*. Briefly summarized, they state,

> Make of yourself a light. Rely upon yourself; do not depend upon anyone else. Make my teachings your light. Rely upon them; do not depend upon any other teaching.[1]

This, we are told, is the final teaching of Gautama Buddha. I believe that these words reveal the fundamental principles of Buddhism.

Here Gautama Buddha instructs each human being to live by relying upon himself or herself. None of us has chosen on our own to live this human life. We have each been born into this world—into a life that utterly transcends

The Shin Buddhist Path

our own wills, a life that has been given to us. We have each appeared in this world, bearing our own sets of problems, yet in a manner not determined by our own wills. This is the real beginning of our human lives: they are filled with contradiction and suffering. Nevertheless, Gautama Buddha teaches us that, no matter how much or what kind of contradiction or suffering we may face, we must take full responsibility to stand up and bear the burden of our own lives, as if we had in fact chosen or even requested those lives. This is the meaning of the words, "Make of yourself a light. Rely upon yourself."

He then turns to his own teachings. The dharma, he says, is the universal principle that pervades the world, all humanity, and, more broadly, the universe itself. In this world, at all times and in all places, there exists a universal principle that holds true for all humans and can be understood by anyone. The Buddha teaches us to live our lives in reliance on this universal principle, making it our light. This is the meaning of, "Make my teachings your light. Rely upon them."

Let us discuss this in a way that may be a little easier to understand, by viewing it in terms of vertical and horizontal axes. The instruction to take responsibility for our own lives may be said to represent a vertical axis. The dharma —the universal principle that pervades the world and all humanity—would then be a horizontal axis. Gautama

Buddha instructs us to live at the point at which the vertical axis and the horizontal axis intersect.

That is to say, we humans all have our own egos. As a result, we always make judgments and act according to whatever is most convenient to ourselves. It is only because there is a universal principle that permeates our lives that we become able to live truly as human beings. That is to say, we must take responsibility for our own lives and bear the responsibility for our lives resolutely; and yet, at the same time, we must be in accord with the universal principle that pervades everything in our lives. The truth is, however, that our lives are always far removed from this point of intersection. For that reason, Gautama Buddha teaches us that we must constantly strive to live at that point.

Gautama was the first person to stand at this point of intersection. Therefore, he was called the "Buddha." He then taught us that we should also try to stand at that point in the same way.

What Is the Buddha?

What then does "Buddha" mean? That is the question that we will take up next.

The word "Buddha" is derived from the Sanskrit word *budh*, which means "to awaken." The verb "to awaken" is

The Shin Buddhist Path

converted into the noun "awakened person" or "awakened one." Thus, "Buddha" indicates an "awakened person."

Next, let me briefly discuss the meaning of "awakening." In Buddhism, a person's intellectual or mental activity is referred to as either "consciousness" (*chishiki* in Japanese) or as "wisdom" (*chie*). The original Sanskrit word for consciousness is *vijñāna*, while the original word for wisdom is *prajñā*. In Buddhism, human "knowing" can be generally divided into these two functions.

Consciousness refers to our normal mental activity. For example, take the case in which we see a flower. Intellectually, the "I" that sees and the flower that is seen arise in a relationship in which each stands in opposition to, and separate from, one another. In addition, when we usually see something in the ordinary sense, we have some kind of subjective reaction to it. For instance, we may feel, "I don't like tulips!" or "I love carnations!" Our own subjective feelings come up to the surface. For the most part, when we human beings see something, we look at it in that way.

There is another way that people see things, which is more purely objective. It differs from the subjective way of looking at things. For instance, the scientific method is supposed to eliminate our feelings of liking or disliking the things that we observe. We may wonder about what flower family the tulip belongs to or where its habitat may be located. With this method of observation, we seek to analyze, synthesize, and comprehend things from many different angles in an objective, scientific way.

The first way of "knowing" encompasses both our ordinary, everyday way of seeing things and the scientific manner of observing objects. In both cases, it is based on a relationship between the subject, which sees, and the object, which is seen. In Buddhism, this way of looking at things is called consciousness (*vijñāna*). In contrast, in wisdom (*prajñā*), the object that is seen and the subject that sees become one. For instance, I become the tulip and the tulip becomes me. That which sees and that which is seen become completely one. This second way of perceiving an object, such as our tulip, is called wisdom. It is also referred to as "awakening" or "realization," and it represents another structure of knowing by human beings.

What does it mean that the object that is seen by the subject and the subject that sees the object become one? When we deeply look into a thing, the "I" that sees becomes —in and of itself—the thing that is seen. As we see the tulip, we enter into the life of that flower. Becoming one with the life of the tulip, we come to know the tulip and see the tulip. Conversely stated, the life of the tulip reaches into our lives and into the deepest part of our hearts and minds. There, we ourselves come to know that tulip's heart and mind, as well as its life and the meaning of its existence. This way of seeing is called "awakening."

For instance, at the front of a flower shop we may see scores of tulips bundled for sale and observe that each flower has been marked with the same price. This is how we look at the tulips using our ordinary way of thinking. Certainly, whether they are white, red, or yellow, tulips of the same variety and size would be priced the same. However, from the standpoint of the life of the tulip itself, the existence and value of each tulip would be utterly unique.

Each and every tulip flower has an irreplaceable life; existing this one time only, it has survived the long winter and is now blooming with all its might. Each and every tulip is blooming at the risk of its own life, so to say that all the flowers are the same would mean that we do not truly see the unique life of the individual tulip. That tulip is blossoming with irreplaceable life. When we are able to see the tulip at the place where the life of the tulip and our own life become one, then for the first time we will be able to see the world of that life, in which each and every tulip is blooming with all of its might. That is the way of seeing that I am talking about now.

According to the Buddhist teachings, when we consume a living thing—such as when we eat the meat of animals such as fish, chicken, or cattle, or when we eat eggs—we are committing the terrible offense of taking life. Because of that special customs have been passed down among Buddhist followers whereby they either never eat such things or they occasionally refrain from eating them. This teaching that the taking of the life of a living thing is a great evil offense is based on the perspective of that living thing. It takes the standpoint of awakening or wisdom (*prajñā*) in which we see that the life of that living thing and our own lives are one. It is born out of a re-examining of our own lives, based on that standpoint. In this way, Buddhism teaches us that all living beings alike live precious, invaluable lives. Thus, all varieties of living things —fish, birds, and humans—have lives of infinite value.

The Buddhist teachings include the notion of *sattva*, a Sanskrit word that is generally applied to all living beings and animals, including human beings. In China it was translated as *shujō*, which refers to the multitude of living beings, or as *ujō*, which indicates things having any kind of feelings. All of these words point to the non-differentiation of all living beings. This kind of thinking arose from the way of seeing that is grounded in the standpoint of awakening in which one sees an object when the subject and the object have become one, and the seer has entered into the object.

This way of seeing things eventually made its way into China, where it was expanded to include not just animals, but also all plant life. That is to say, daikon, potatoes, carrots, and so on all contain the same life as that of human beings. This gave rise to the thought that our own life, the life of a daikon, or the life of a carrot should all be understood as sharing common value. Broadening that understanding somewhat more, in the lives of all living beings one discovers the fundamental, common nature of all life. In Japanese Buddhism, this way of thinking eventually merged with traditional Japanese thought. Life came to be viewed very broadly, extending beyond plants and animals even to minerals, so that life could be detected even in a small pebble. Even there we can find a life that is in common with our own. This was the result of the gradual development of the notion of wisdom (awakening and realization) in Indian Buddhism.

We will not examine this subject in any greater depth at this time. However, one could say that this way of looking at things, based in Buddhist wisdom, whereby we see an object by becoming that object and transcend the opposition between subject and object, is an example of Eastern thought. It is the complete opposite of scientific thinking as it has arisen in the West. I believe, moreover, that, as the destruction of the environment worsens and we reach a point of crisis in which the very future of our planet is at rish, this way of seeing things based on Buddhist wisdom can be very important, for it can make possible a new kind of human life in the twenty-first century. This unique kind of human knowing arises in the sphere of an extremely profound mind, that is, in the world of spirituality. This is the significance of wisdom and awakening today.

We must seek to stand at the point of intersection of the vertical axis of self-responsibility and the horizontal axis of the universal principle of the dharma. If we do so our lives will become focused on seeing things with the eyes of wisdom and awakening. Buddhism teaches us that a life of awakening is the ideal way to live as a person of the world and the human race.

Aim of the Buddhist Teachings

The Buddhist teaching is intended to enable us to cultivate this kind of awakening within ourselves. When we are able to cultivate even just a small amount of wisdom, we become human beings in the truest sense. That is to say, in awakening we subjectively engage in true human growth. We personally cast off our old human skin and become the kinds of persons that we are capable of being.

Normally, we lead self-centered lives, wearing the skin of ego-attachment. Typically we think, "I like her; I hate him. She is my friend; he is my enemy." In a variety of ways we reject some persons, while accepting others. And yet, as we do away with this way of looking at things, even little by little, or, as we come to grasp objects directly, without making them into objectified or scientific abstractions, we will come to see objects by becoming one with them. As we learn this Buddhist way of seeing things our current self-centered ways of living and ways of being will be constantly called into question.

In this sense, the Buddhist path indicates an ongoing process in which our own self-centered ways of living are constantly being examined and the old skin of those lives is being cast off. Further, casting off the old skin means, at the same time, that we are growing into and becoming our new selves.

As we cast off, we become; as we become, we cast off. The process of casting off our old selves and becoming our new selves, becoming and casting off, continues on and on without end. This idea helps us to understand whether we can indeed come close to standing at the point of intersection of the vertical and horizontal axes, which we saw earlier. In our actual state, we learn, it is impossible for us to reach that point. We are not able to cast off our old skin and realize growth, as we might like. However, we can aim for that, and as we earnestly learn the dharma, we will be constantly brought under severe scrutiny for as long as we live. This, I believe, is the basic aim of the Buddhist teachings.

Buddhism calls the current state of our existence into

question and teaches us the true way to live as human beings. As a result, each of us undergoes a change, for we are made to realize personal, subjective growth. Let me say this in a different way: as we learn the Buddha-dharma, we who are *not so* become *so*, little by little. As we question ourselves, we gradually nurture ourselves. This is the basic character of the Buddhist teachings.

Therefore, Buddhism is different from other religions. Other religions may first discuss and acknowledge the existence of God as an absolute being. They then teach that people must live in relationship with that absolute God. Buddhism, however, is not founded on any dualistic conception of human beings and an absolute being. What Buddhism teaches is that, as we learn the dharma—the universal principle that pervades the world and the universe—we come to question, through the dharma, the state of our own existence and exhaustively search for our own ideal way of being. In this way, we who are *not so* learn to become *so*. This is the teaching of Gautama Buddha.

The Development of Buddhism

Buddhism after the Death of Gautama Buddha

Soon after the death of Gautama Buddha, Buddhism divided into two main streams. The first stream was

The Shin Buddhist Path

renunciant monk-centered Buddhism. This type of Buddhism was for persons who wished to emulate Gautama. By renouncing their homes and leaving the secular world, they sought to walk the same path that Gautama had followed during his life. The other main stream was lay householder-centered Buddhism. This form of Buddhism was for lay householders, who devoted themselves to supporting the lifestyles of Gautama and his disciples.

Stated simply, renunciant Buddhists worked to compile Gautama Buddha's teachings precisely as he had left them. They then concentrated on learning those teachings correctly so that they might be passed on accurately to succeeding generations. Renunciant Buddhism focused on the teachings of Gautama and its development took place around those scriptures.

In contrast, after the death of Gautama Buddha, lay supporters endeavored to cremate his remains, in accordance with his dying wishes. Those cremated remains (Sārira) were divided into eight portions, and believers brought them back to their respective homes. There they constructed *stūpa* in which the remains could be enshrined. It might be said, therefore, that *stūpa*—portions of which still exist in India today—were originally gravesites built to enshrine Gautama Buddha's remains. In householder Buddhism, lay followers learned the teachings of the

Buddha by focusing on the *stūpa*.

Renunciant Buddhism

The Buddhist teaching also refers to an awakened person or Buddha as a *tathāgata*. The word *tathāgata* is a combination of two Sanskrit words, *tatha* and *gata*, and also *tatha* and *agata*. Tatha has the meaning of "truth" or "suchness." It refers to the ultimate value that human beings should aim to realize. In other words, *tatha* has the same meaning as enlightenment or awakening. The meaning of the word gata is "went" or "departed."

It follows that *tathāgata* (*tatha* + *gata*) means that one has gone to or departed toward truth and suchness. In China this word was translated as *nyoko* (thus gone; gone to thusness). This is how Gautama Buddha was understood by Buddhist renunciants. To them, Gautama was "thus gone"; he had gone forward to and departed toward truth, suchness, and ultimate value. Hence, it was thought, one also must try to learn without error the path that Gautama Buddha established and follow in his footsteps. This was the teaching of renunciant monks.

Naturally, this kind of approach to Buddhism would involve a life of extremely difficult religious practice. Renunciant monks all made diligent efforts to perform practices, cultivate their minds, and earnestly engage the path for the attainment of Buddhahood. Such Buddhist teachings maintained that such practitioners would be able to attain Buddhahood, realizing wisdom, awakening, or enlightenment in the midst of this life and in this present body. This kind of renunciant-centered approach became one stream of Buddhism in India, China, and Japan. It would later come to be called the teaching of the "Path of Sages."

Householder Buddhism

However, another, distinct understanding regarding Gautama Buddha also arose. In this stream of thought, the word *tathāgata* was taken to be a combination of the words tatha and agata. In the word *agata*, the prefix "a" signifies negation. Since it negates the word *gata* ("has gone"), it means, on the contrary, "has come." It follows that *tathāgata* (*tatha* + *agata*) signifies that truth or suchness has come here. In China, this word was translated as *nyorai* (thus come; comes from thusness). Here, then, Gautama Buddha is understood to be "thus come." It is not that he has gone off to the truth. On the contrary, he has come to us from truth in order to teach us to become Buddhas.

This kind of understanding was gleaned by people who focused solely on the stupa, which enshrined the remains of Gautama Buddha, for it allowed them to continuously call to mind his virtues and extol his character. This understanding then became widespread among lay householders-people who continued to dwell in worldly life, who humbly engaged in farming and trade, and who worked diligently in everyday life, while remaining enmeshed in all sorts of ego-attachments.

To those living a lay householder's life, it never occurred to them that they should be able to look upon Gautama Buddha as their predecessor or to follow in his footsteps. Instead, they came to see Gautama as truth or suchness itself, which came from beyond and appeared over here in order to teach them. They came to think of Gautama Buddha as their savior, who actively approached this world in order to save them. This stream of householder Buddhism was also transmitted through India, China, and Japan, and later came to be called the "Pure Land teachings."

The idea of Amida Buddha arose out of this kind of householder Buddhism. Although it was deemed possible to realize awakening in the midst of the current state of human life, it was completely unthinkable that lay householders, who were mired in the secular world, could attain Buddhahood in this life. Instead it was taught that, no matter how deep one's karmic sins might be, one who followed Gautama's teachings, aimed toward truth or suchness, and lived one's life with singleness of purpose

The Shin Buddhist Path

would upon death be able to attain birth in the Pure Land without fail. There for the first time one would attain Buddhahood. Here was the unique character of the Buddhist teachings for lay householders, the Pure Land teachings of Amida Buddha.

Formation of the Pure Land Teachings

It is believed that this approach to the Buddhist teachings—that is, the idea of Amida Buddha—arose around the first century C.E., approximately four to five hundred years after the death of Gautama Buddha. Today, there are many questions regarding the circumstances of its formation. However, on the whole, it is believed that the formation of this new Buddhism for the sake of the lay householder masses was influenced by the Roman and Grecian cultures of the West. The base of its development is thought to have been in the area of Gandhara, an important post along the trade routes between Rome and China, located in the Indus River basin of Northwest India (present-day Pakistan).

These two streams of Indian Buddhism—the Path of Sages centered on renunciant monks and the Pure Land teachings centered on lay householders—eventually flowed into China and Japan. Of the two, the teachings of the Path of Sages was considered to be a superior form of Buddhism, since it taught practitioners to adopt the renunciant lifestyle of Gautama Buddha, leave their homes, seriously perform practices, attain awakening, and become Buddhas in this life. In contrast, the Pure Land teachings focused on lay householders, and even among them, it was intended for people who were socially and economically destitute. It could be learned by foolish beings who were incapable of storing up roots of good or even by those whose karmic sins were heavy and profound. Thus, the Pure Land teachings were considered to be an extremely low-level and inferior form of Buddhism. This opinion was long held within the various streams of Japanese Buddhism.

However, this kind of thinking was completely turned upside down by Hōnen, a practitioner of Buddhism during the Kamakura period of Japan.

Hōnen and the Pure Land Teachings

While on Mt. Hiei, Hōnen had been deeply engaged in the study of the teachings of the Path of Sages. However, he came to realize how difficult it actually was to realize awakening and attain Buddhahood during one's life. In the midst of despair, however, he was able to open his eyes to a completely new way of thinking. That is to say, he came to realize that the teachings of the Path of Sages, the high-level Buddhist understanding centered on renunciant

The Shin Buddhist Path

monks, in fact taught that only people of special character and abilities would be able to attain Buddhahood. And even such persons could do so only after continuously performing religious practices in the depths of the mountains, a lifestyle that actually required the support of many others. Under those conditions, only a limited number of people would be able to access that path.

Hōnen became conscious of the fact that that kind of Buddhism could not have been the focus of the teaching of Gautama Buddha. Did Gautama not teach that all living things, and not just human beings but even all animals, would attain Buddhahood? Is that not what he had aspired for? The Pure Land teachings, Hōnen learned, taught of a path upon which all lay believers, and even those who committed all sorts of karmic evil in the midst of the harshness of everyday life, could equally attain Buddhahood. As such, it was a path accessible to all people, and it enabled all people to grow into true human beings. This Pure Land teaching, he thought, must in fact have been the true Buddhist teaching expounded by Gautama Buddha.

Again, the prevailing opinion at the time was that the teachings of the Path of Sages, which described an extremely difficult path and taught that only a few skilled renunciant monks would be able to master it successfully, was the most superior, highest—grade Buddhist teaching. Such a path, it was held, constituted the central import of

Gautama Buddha's teaching. In contrast, Hōnen took the position that it was the Pure Land teachings, which revealed a path upon which all persons—no matter how foolish one might be or what kind of karmic offenses one might commit—can attain Buddhahood, which transmitted the true heart and mind of Gautama Buddha. His stance represented a complete reversal of the prevailing understanding of the Buddhist teachings, for he held that the Pure Land teachings represented the most superior, true Buddhist teaching. That was Hōnen's understanding of the Pure Land teachings.

When Shinran met Hōnen, he was able to come in contact with the heart and mind of Gautama Buddha, with the true Buddhist teaching, for the first time. That is why he was willing to risk all to learn from his teacher. Under Hōnen's guidance, Shinran poured over the Pure Land Buddhist scriptures that spoke of Amida Buddha and studied the many texts of the Pure Land masters of India, China, and Japan. In that way, he was able to comprehend the fundamental purport of the Pure Land teachings and the idea of Amida Buddha.

This completes our brief look at the fundamental principles of the Buddhist teachings that were expounded by Gautama Buddha, as well as the way in which those Buddhist teachings reached Shinran in Japan.

The Pure Land Buddhist Path

Amida Buddha

Next, we will look at the experience of awakening and the path to the attainment of Buddhahood as they are discussed in Pure Land Buddhism. Let us start by thinking about the Buddha named "Amida."

In the language of ancient India, "Amida Buddha" was called by two names, "*Amitābha*" and "*Amitāyus*." It is believed that the name "Amida" was a later development of those words. As I mentioned earlier, the prefix "*a*" negates the word that follows it. The word "*mita*" means "to be measured or reckoned." Thus, "*a* + *mita*" means "not to be measured" or "immeasurable." "*Abha*" refers to light, while "*ayus*" refers to lifespan. Therefore, Amida Buddha is the Buddha possessed of unlimited light and an unlimited span of life.

Let me explain this a little bit more. *Amitābha* (immeasurable light) is also a way of expressing spatial infinity. From a point of origin within the eternal present, light streams out, limitlessly, into space. And just like the light of the sun, this light illuminates all darkness. It reveals for us which paths are false, and points us to the correct path that we ought to follow. *Amitābha* symbolizes the activity of infinite light, which streams out in countless directions.

Amitāyus (immeasurable life) indicates life that is infinite in span and continues throughout time, without break or limit. It also refers to eternity, which is without beginning or end. Here, the idea that life is infinite implies that life constantly sacrifices itself in order to nurture new life. It is just like a plant that withers and decays so as to become the compost that will nourish a new sprout, or like a parent who curtails her own life so that her child may realize full growth. "Immeasurable life" symbolizes this activity of nurturing true life, activity that is directed to all living things. Thus, Amida Buddha signifies that which illuminates and nurtures all people and all living things across infinite space and infinite time.

The Shin Buddhist Path

Immortalization of Gautama Buddha

The expressions amitābha and amitāyus are also connected to Gautama Buddha, whose life stories, produced after his death, often praise him as being one possessed of unlimited light and unlimited life. Gautama Buddha's life in this world came to an end when he was eighty years old. Yet, the teaching, or dharma, that he expounded represents a universal principle that pervades the world, reaching all places and remaining valid in all periods of time. Accordingly, both his teachings and his life are praised as being eternal. Spatially, they extend out to guide all people without exception, and temporally, they approach people and turn them toward an infinite future.

This view of Gautama Buddha was adopted by lay householders. It slowly moved in the direction from the historical to the abstract, wherein Gautama Buddha came to be viewed more as a symbol of transcendence and eternity. Finally, it gave rise to the idea of Amida Buddha as an autonomous Buddha, one of immeasurable light and immeasurable life that transcended even the human Gautama. These were the historical circumstances that led to the formation of the notion of Amida Buddha.

We might say that Amida Buddha arose within the sincerity of the hearts and minds of people who praised and revered Gautama Buddha after his death. The notion of

Amida Buddha was formed through the process of a gradual abstraction both of Gautama's life and of the inner reality of his experience of awakening—his enlightenment as a Buddha—which he fulfilled at the risk of his own subjectivity. This was symbolized as Amida Buddha, the Buddha of immeasurable light and life, the Buddha possessed of infinite reach throughout space and unlimited connectivity throughout all time.

Amida Buddha as Symbol

In India long ago there was a Buddhist follower by the name of Nāgārjuna (ca. 150-250 C.E.), who had such a deep understanding of the Buddhist teaching that he was called the "second Gautama." In his text, the *Commentary on the Mahāprajñāpāramitā Sutra*, he discusses the Buddhist teachings using the imagery of a finger and the moon. The moon gleams high in the heavens of the night sky. We ordinary beings, however, are always looking downward as we walk about and so we do not look up into the sky. The teaching of the Buddha is like a person who taps us on the shoulder and, pointing to the moon with his finger, urges us to look up at it.

The teachings of Buddhism and the words that express correspond to the finger in this illustration. The moon, which glitters high in the distant sky far beyond the finger,

The Shin Buddhist Path

represents the ultimate value of truth or suchness; it is the awakening or enlightenment that Gautama Buddha experienced himself. Between the finger and the moon lies a vast distance. As a result, we are able to see the moon for the first time only because of the finger—in concrete terms, only through the words of the teaching expounded by Gautama, or through the human personality of those who have learned the teaching and walked the path before us.

If we were to look up into the heavens on our own, we might not be able to recognize the moon. Without question, there must be a finger—the dharma or a person who can relate it to us—that can teach us about the moon. For us, the story of Amida Buddha is that finger. The entire teaching of Amida Buddha is the finger, but that teaching is not Amida Buddha itself. All of the many teachings that expound Amida Buddha constitute the finger. The realm of awakening or enlightenment, which Gautama Buddha realized in his life, as well as ultimate truth and value, constitute the moon.

The teachings of Buddhism are always expressed by the relationship between the finger and the moon, between the words of the teachings (the finger) and suchness or truth itself (the moon), which is the essence of those teachings. Therefore, we must not think that we are able to understand Buddhism or realize *shinjin* simply by studying the words of the teachings and knowing about them in our heads. That would be a complete mistake. It would be nothing more than believing that we are looking at the moon, when in reality we are only seeing the finger. As we study the teachings and look at the finger, we must turn our eyes toward the moon, which is gleaming in the distance far away from the finger.

What fills up the gap between the finger and the moon is our individual practice on the Buddhist path. Our engagement of the path enables us to realize the experience of awakening, in which the Buddhist teachings become a personal matter for us. If we do not live in this way or if we do not walk the path at the risk of our very selves, then we will never reach the world of awakening, which is the aim of Buddhism. This must be clearly understood as we learn the teaching of Amida Buddha.

Shinran addressed this teaching of Nāgārjuna in his own writings. However, traditional Shin Buddhist doctrine is not clear on this point, and often confounds the finger and the moon. We must also be fully aware of this.

Once again, the teaching of Amida Buddha is a finger pointing to the moon of enlightenment. And, to the extent that they are discussed with words, the Primal Vow and the Name of Amida are merely fingers as well. They are not the moon. This point is clearly taught by Shinran.

In religious studies, such things are referred to as symbols. In this regard, it is worth noting the approach to symbols taken by the Christian theologian Paul Tillich (1886-1965). According to Tillich, the finger corresponds to a symbol. It is through this symbol that the ultimate can be made clear. At the same time the ultimate moves as a symbol toward the present situation. That is, a symbol points from the ground to the sky, or from the secular world to the transcendent realm. In addition, the transcendent realm discloses itself as a symbol to the secular world.

Nāgārjuna was saying the same thing. We are able to see the moon because of the finger. However, it is because of the light of the moon that we are able to see the finger and the finger is able to function as a finger. The finger is something connected to this earth, and yet at the same time it is also an extension of the light of the moon. In other words, the teaching—as symbol—points toward ultimate value and truth, which transcends this secular world. Conversely, that which transcends this secular world also draws near to this world.

Earlier I explained that *tathāgata* means both "gone to thusness" and "comes from thusness." I mentioned that Gautama Buddha had "gone to thusness" when he departed from this world and went to suchness. Lay believers who revered Gautama, however, understood it to be that Gautama "comes from thusness"; that is, he approaches us from beyond. There is much in that discussion that overlaps with this one.

The teaching elucidating Amida Buddha is like a finger pointing to the moon. As a symbol it points from the secular world toward truth itself and ultimate value that transcends the secular world. However, the truth, as the moon itself, also comes to this secular world. It moves in two directions at the same time: both "gone to thusness" and "comes from thusness."

We have seen that the idea of the Buddha "Amida" evolved as those who cherished the memory of Gautama Buddha, a human being who was born in India around the fourth century B.C.E., went on to immortalize both the person Gautama and the reality of his enlightenment experience as infinite light and life. Accordingly, the image of Amida Buddha, which we now worship, is a symbolic representation of the figure of Gautama Buddha. The point here is that, even as Amida Buddha was "produced" by Gautama Buddha, at the same time, in an even more profound way, Amida Buddha "appeared" as Gautama Buddha. The idea of Amida Buddha thus arose from two directions. First, it went from the secular world to the transcendent (*tathāgata* as "gone to thusness"). Conversely, it moved from the transcendent to the secular world (*tathāgata* as "comes from thusness"). I believe that this must be the fundamental understanding of Amida Buddha in Shin Buddhism.

Jinen

Shinran's understanding of Amida Buddha can be seen in his grasp of the word *jinen*. At the end of his eighty-sixth year, a few years before passing away at the age of ninety, Shinran wrote a letter to one of his principal disciples, Kenshin, in which he says,

> Amida Buddha fulfills the purpose of making us know the significance of jinen.[2]

The Chinese characters 自然, when read as "*jinen*," have a very special meaning. In particular, Shinran indicates here that both *ji* and *nen* reveal transcendent truth or ultimate value. He comprehended *jinen*, a word that originated in Chinese Buddhist thought, essentially as "being without color and having no form." In terms of the illustration of the finger and the moon, *jinen* would correspond to the moon. Amida Buddha, on the other hand, clarifies this transcendent truth, or ultimate value, which is without color or form, so that we may be able to understand it. Returning to our illustration, Amida Buddha corresponds to the finger pointing to the moon.

In Shinran's phrase "the significance of *jinen*," the Chinese character for "significance" is written as 様 (*yō* in modern Japanese). This has the meaning of form, appearance, aspect, state, or circumstances. In his phrase "fulfills the purpose of making us know," we find the word "re-u," which would be written as 料 (*ryō* in modern Japanese). This word refers to the material, factor, or element that enables us to know something. As a result, Amida Buddha is simply the material—the finger—that enables us to know ultimate truth that is formless, colorless, and transcends this world.

In other words, Amida Buddha fulfills the purpose of making us know the transcendent, ultimate realm of the enlightenment experienced by Gautama Buddha. This is the way in which Shinran spoke of Amida Buddha.

Let us think a little bit more about *jinen*. The usual Japanese reading of the Chinese character 自 (*ji*) is "*mizukara*," which refers to "me" or "myself." However, Shinran did not grasp it in this way at all. Instead, he read it as "*onozukara*." When read as "*mizukara*," the character would indicate something very self-centered. It would point to an image of myself that is hardened with a sense of ego. When this ego, however, is relentlessly brought into question and thereby completely crushed, then a new self, a self transcending the ego, will be born. Buddhism refers to this self that transcends the ego as "non-self," or the self that is "not-the-self." Buddhism also calls this the "great self," which indicates that it is the infinitely great self, the self of unlimited reach.

The Shin Buddhist Path

What does this mean? Let us return to our earlier discussion of the tulip. Whenever we look at a tulip, we do so in a self-centered way. For instance, we may say, "That flower is tall," "It is cheap," "I don't like it," or "I like it." However, if we abandon our self-centered egos and come to realize "non-self" or "great self," then we will see the tulip by entering into the tulip itself. We will see the tulip by taking in the life of the tulip and becoming the tulip itself. We are able to truly see another when we become free of our egos and realize "non-self." Stating it conversely, we can truly see all things when we become "great self" and take all things as ourselves, enveloping them all. "Non-self" is the negative way of expressing this. "Great self" is simply the affirmative way of saying it. That is to say, "*onozukara*" refers to the self that has become "non-self" or "great self." It reveals another self that has become free of ego-attachment and has cast away the skin of one's old self. This is the meaning of the word "*ji*" in *jinen*.

Next, let us think about the meaning of the word 然 (*nen*) in *jinen*. Originally, the term meant "to become so" ("*shikaru*" in Japanese). This connoted a shift of some sort, whereby a thing changes into something else. However, Shinran read "*nen*" in the passive voice so that it would mean "to be made so" ("*shikarashimu*"). We have previously seen that *onozukara* refers to "non-self," which is "not-the-self," or "great self," which stretches out infinitely.

It is transcendent and ultimate truth, the world of suchness that is without color or form. It is the self that is free of all ego-attachment, and therefore has infinite breadth. Inevitably, then, it is constantly reaching out without rest in the direction of all living beings and all things. This ceaseless working of "non-self" or "great self" (*ji, onozukara*) reaches all beings, allowing them "to be made so" (*nen, shikarashimu*). This is the meaning of *jinen*, which Shinran read as "*onozukara shikarashimu.*" Amida Buddha is the material that enables us to know this truth of jinen.

Wisdom and Compassion

We will now take a look at Amida Buddha from a different angle by taking up Shinran's understanding of wisdom and compassion.

Wisdom (*prajñā* in Sanskrit; *chie* in Japanese) is an activity of knowing, which we described earlier as awakening. It is a mental activity in which both subject and object become one in mutual identity. That is to say, the object that is seen becomes, in and of itself, the subject or self that sees; and the self as subject that sees becomes, in and of itself, the object itself that is seen. The activity of wisdom or awakening, as the oneness of subject and object, means that one knows a thing by becoming the thing.

Returning once again to our example of the tulip, we come to know the tulip by becoming the very tulip itself. None of the tulips on display at the flower shop are the same. In reality, each and every tulip is blossoming to the utmost with irreplaceable life. Wisdom is the way of seeing each tulip by assuming the standpoint of each and every tulip. Inevitably, the life of each tulip is bestowed with unlimited value and care, and an aspiration to nurture that life eternally arises.

At the very place and time that a subject sees an object by becoming it, there is also born an activity that seeks to extend the life of that object, as well as the meaning of its existence, and enable it to go on living as itself eternally. This activity is called compassion (*maitrī* and *karuṇā* in Sanskrit; *jihi* in Japanese). *Maitrī* (*ji*) has the meaning of "friendliness," "intimate feelings of fellowship," and "close connections." *Karuṇā* (*hi*) indicates "pity," "sympathy," and "feelings of deep compassion." Thus, wisdom and compassion represent two aspects of a single activity. *Jinen*, on the other hand, unifies these two aspects into one. Further, they might also be connected in this way: *ji* ("non-self" or "great self") corresponds to wisdom (*prajñā*), while *nen* ("to be made so") is equivalent to compassion (*maitrī* and *karuṇā*).

As I mentioned earlier, Amida Buddha, as explained in the Pure Land teachings, is a symbol of the realm of the ultimate experience of enlightenment, which Gautama Buddha himself attained. That experience is also addressed more concretely by such ideas as *jinen* or wisdom and compassion. It can also be explained in the following way: truth is always distinct from non-truth, and thus it is always far removed from non-truth. However, because truth is truth, it will necessarily move toward non-truth.

Truth is distinct from non-truth and falsity, and yet if truth were estranged from non-truth, so as to exclude it, saying "Non-truth, do not come close to me!" or "Falsity, be gone!" then it could not be called authentic truth. Authentic truth is infinitely free and distinct from falsity. At the same time, it is always concerned for that falsity. It feels falsity's pain within itself. It has deep lamentation and pity for it. It also aspires to cultivate and transform falsity so that it becomes true, like itself. Is that not the authentic meaning of truth? As I have stated before, in Buddhism ultimate truth or enlightenment has infinite concern for those who have not yet awakened to truth. It feels pity for those who are deluded and seeks to draw near to them. Enlightenment always involves this kind of activity.

The original meaning of pity, or *karuṇā* (*hi*), is "to groan." To groan means that, even though we may try to endure suffering stoically, the pain becomes just too much for us to bear, and so our voices cry out in anguish. Ultimate truth is groaning constantly. Ever groaning over our suffering, it is always coming nearer and nearer to us, who are false and deluded. That is also the meaning of Amida Buddha.

Buddha-Body and Buddha-Name

The Buddhist sutras, then, teach us that ultimate truth, which is "gone to thusness" or jinen, constantly approaches us and manifests itself concretely in the secular world as that which "comes from thusness." In the sutras, this approach of truth is symbolically represented in two senses.

In the first sense, Amida Buddha comes to us as language or as a word. In the second, Amida Buddha approaches us as form. Both ways of understanding can be seen in the Indian Pure Land sutras, particularly the *Larger Sutra of Immeasurable Life*, the *Contemplation Sutra*, and the *Amida Sutra*. Those sutras reveal that Amida-as-word comes to us concretely as the Buddha's Name, "Namu Amida Butsu." Amida-as-form approaches us as the body of Amida Buddha. These are the two ways in which Amida Buddha's appearance is symbolically represented in the sutras.

In order for Amida Buddha to be comprehended as a word, it must be heard. That is to say, Amida-as-word can and must be heard by us. Amida Buddha comes close to us, by "naming itself." By taking a name, it reveals itself to us as a word and as a voice. The only way that we can encounter Amida Buddha is by hearing Amida naming itself. Hence, "hearing the Name" is an important element of the path for encountering the Buddha.

On the other hand, in order for Amida Buddha to be comprehended as form or "Buddha-body," we must be able to see the Buddha. That is to say, the only way for us to encounter Amida-as-form is to visualize Amida Buddha intently. In this case, then, "contemplating or visualizing the Buddha" is the path for encountering the Buddha. Actually, "hearing the Name" and "seeing the Buddha" do not simply mean that we hear with our physical ears or see with our physical eyes. Instead, "hearing the Name" means that we must make the ears of our minds clear and serene, so that we can focus on and hear the voice of the Buddha naming itself. "Seeing the Buddha" means that we must open the eyes of our minds, so that we can contemplate and visualize the form of that Buddha.

Many Pure Land Buddhist sutras teach of Amida Buddha. From the time that Pure Land Buddhism developed in China, however, its principal sutras have been the following three: the *Larger Sutra of Immeasurable Life*, the *Contemplation Sutra*, and the *Amida Sutra*. Many Pure Land sutras explain Amida Buddha to be either the Buddha-name or the Buddha-body. In contrast, both the *Larger Sutra* and the *Amida Sutra* essentially grasp Amida Buddha

The Shin Buddhist Path

as the Name. Accordingly, both sutras state that the path of "hearing the Name," the path of hearing Amida Buddha revealing itself as the Name, is the way for us to encounter Amida Buddha. The *Contemplation Sutra*, on the other hand, chiefly comprehends Amida Buddha as the Buddha-body. Hence, this sutra teaches us that we can encounter Amida Buddha by taking the path of "seeing the Buddha," the path of contemplating the Buddha's body.

The Primal Vow of Amida Buddha

As we have seen, truth that transcends this world must necessarily approach and manifest itself in this world. The Pure Land sutras elucidate this idea through the teaching of the Primal Vow of Amida Buddha.

Truth and Non-truth

The word "Primal Vow" (*hongan* in Japanese) is based on the original Sanskrit word "*pūrva-praṇidhāna*." *Pūrva* has the sense of "to precede" or "before," and thus means "past" or "past life." It also has the implication "as a necessary consequence." Therefore, it refers to the necessary or inevitable consequence of truth itself, working since the infinite or beginningless past. *Praṇidhāna* means "effort, endeavor, diligence, or arduous effort." It has also been translated as "wish," "aspiration," or "vow." It follows that *pūrva-praṇidhāna* refers to a "vow from the past" or an "original, or primal, vow."

Praṇidhāna has been rendered as 願 (*gan*) in Chinese scriptures. As mentioned above, this word has often been translated as "vow." However, its original meaning was that of "hard, firm, or steadfast" ("*katai*" in Japanese). Thinking along those lines, it means that Amida Buddha's Primal Vow is very hard and steadfast; it has not crumbled or declined, but continues to exist as it has since the infinite past. "Hard" may seem to be a strange expression, so let us take this a bit further.

The Chinese character gan can also be read in Japanese as "*negai*," which means "aspiration, wish, or vow." There are a variety of interpretations of that character as well. One of them states that the portion "*ne*" comes from the character 音 meaning "sound." That is, negai signifies that one wishes for something as one cries and raises one's voice. "*Ne*" may also be said to come from the character 根, which means "root." Thus, "*negai*" means that one raises a tree by adding soil and water to its roots.

In the Pure Land teachings Amida Buddha symbolically describes the activity of ultimate truth, which draws near and presents itself to us, who are not true. This activity is further represented by the symbol of the Primal Vow, *pūrva-praṇidhāna*. As a necessary consequence of its being true, it has come to us from the beginningless beginning in order to nurture us to become true. This activity of approach is a very hard or steadfast thing, for it cannot be broken by anything. In addition, out of its deep wish for us, it cries, raises its voice, and works its way close to us, in order to care for us without cease. This has connections with our earlier discussion about wisdom and compassion. Truth, or wisdom (*prajñā*) as compassion (*maitrī* and *karuṇā*), constantly groans for us; it envelops us, who are not true, and never leaves us. Moreover, it seeks to make clear to us that ultimate truth constantly approaches us and reveals itself to us, who are filled with falsity. As it does so, it seeks to transform us, who are not-true and false, to become true.

Amida Buddha's Primal Vow

Amida Buddha's Primal Vow (*pūrva-praṇidhāna*) is expounded in detail in the *Larger Sutra of Immeasurable Life*. An expanded explanation of the Primal Vow involves the idea of the forty-eight Vows. The core of those Vows is the Eighteenth Vow. Although we will discuss the entire content of the Eighteenth Vow, let us consider just a portion of it at this time.

> If, when I attain Buddhahood, the sentient beings of the ten quarters, with sincere mind entrusting

themselves, aspiring to be born in my land, and saying my Name perhaps even ten times, should not be born there, may I not attain the supreme enlightenment.[3]

This passage reveals Amida Buddha's great wish for all living beings, including all animals and plants. It is a wish to guide all beings to the Buddha's realm, the Pure Land, and, once there, to bring them to the attainment of enlightenment, without fail. If, moreover, any living being should be unable to awaken *shinjin* and attain Buddhahood, then Amida Buddha vows not to attain enlightenment or become a Buddha.

In other words, if all living beings do not realize awakening and attain enlightenment, Amida Buddha will also not realize awakening or attain enlightenment. Stated differently, if all living beings do not realize true happiness, then Amida Buddha will absolutely not become a Buddha. The sutra teaches us that this is Amida Buddha's fundamental wish, or Primal Vow.

Let me recast this Vow into more personal terms: if I do not become a Buddha, then Amida will not become a Buddha. Amida will become a Buddha and I will become a Buddha at exactly the same time. My attainment of Buddhahood and Amida's attainment of Buddhahood are simultaneous and mutually identical events. Therefore, they do not each take place separately. This is the logical structure of the Primal Vow. To push this even further, we may also say that my attainment of Buddhahood and Amida's attainment of Buddhahood arise simultaneously within my realization of *shinjin*. In that *shinjin*, I become my true self; in that same *shinjin*, Amida Buddha actually exists as Amida Buddha for me.

Buddha's Enlightenment and Our Enlightenment

Most people have never heard the teaching of Shinran presented in this way before. However, this is just how the *Larger Sutra of Immeasurable Life* presents the logic of Amida Buddha's Primal Vow. Mahayana Buddhist thought holds that the self and the other, or that is, you and I, exist simultaneously.

Let us say, for instance, that at this very moment I am giving a lecture to you. Our relationship is not that I was here first, and then you were here later. Neither is it that you were here first and I was here later. My being here and your being here must take place at the same time. I exist here and now only because of the fact that you are here to listen to my lecture. All of you as well exist here and now as you listen to my lecture. In this sense, my existence and your existence, here and now, come about simultaneously and in mutual identity. In the same way, Amida's attainment of Buddhahood and our attainment of

Buddhahood take place simultaneously and identically within the reality of the Primal Vow of Amida Buddha.

As long as all living beings have not been saved and have not attained enlightenment, Amida will not become a Buddha. However, you might say, the number of living beings is immeasurable, boundless, and infinite. It would follow that, unless the infinite number of living beings all attain Buddhahood, it will not be possible for Amida Buddha to attain enlightenment. Thus, Amida Buddha can never attain Buddhahood! My response to you would be, "Yes. According to such logic, it would be impossible for Amida Buddha to be Amida Buddha!"

It has been said that Amida Buddha originally became a Buddha in the beginningless past. And yet, at the same time, Amida Buddha can never become Amida Buddha. This is a truly contradictory statement. However, as long as Amida Buddha symbolizes the approach of ultimate truth, which discloses itself to the delusion and falsity of the secular world in order to turn delusion and falsity into truth, and as long as delusion and falsity is infinite and immeasurable in this world, this is the only way in which we can describe Amida Buddha.

Over one hundred years ago a scholar offered the following interpretation in order to try to make this thinking more easily understandable: Amida Buddha becomes Amida Buddha each time an individual sentient

The Shin Buddhist Path

being realizes birth in the Pure Land and attains enlightenment. This means that Amida Buddhas exist in proportion to the number of sentient beings. When one person attains birth and realizes Buddhahood, Amida Buddha becomes a Buddha along with that person. Hence, Amida Buddha establishes a Primal Vow for each individual and attains Buddhahood along with that individual. As a result, Amida is constantly attaining Buddhahood, and innumerable Amida Buddhas exist in a number proportional to the number of sentient beings. As we mentioned earlier, this is a way of trying to give a concrete and simple explanation of the mutual identity of our attainment of Buddhahood and Amida's attainment of Buddhahood. That is to say, sentient beings attain enlightenment and Amida Buddha attains enlightenment at precisely the same time.

Eastern Logic and Western Logic

Thus, the salvation of Amida Buddha is not a dualistic concept. It is not a situation whereby Amida Buddha existed somewhere long before there were any people, and now, after his attainment of Buddhahood, calls out to people in order to guide and accompany them to the Pure Land. Such a dualistic notion of salvation is not Mahayana Buddhism.

The Pure Land Buddhist teaching of Amida Buddha is based on the principles of Mahayana Buddhism. Hence, its stance is fundamentally non-dualistic and subjective in nature. Nevertheless, Pure Land Buddhism talks about Amida Buddha in a manner that seems dualistic, objective, and objectifying. Conversely stated, although the Pure Land teachings describe Amida Buddha as some sort of object, at the same time they adopts a subjective and non-dualistic perspective, which states that Amida Buddha does not exist apart from us.

Zen Buddhism talks about the relationship between the Buddha and the self in a direct, non-dualistic way. It takes the position that the self is fundamentally a Buddha; and there is no Buddha aside from the self. As a result, however, Zen is constantly faced with the risk of falling into a kind of abstract idealism. The history of the Zen school shows many instances of that very thing. However, Pure Land Buddhism is non-dualistic even while it sometimes speaks dualistically. And, even while it may use dualistic expressions, it returns to its fundamental, non-dualistic standpoint. This is the unique character of the Pure Land form of Mahayana Buddhism. It is important that we understand this point fully and make no mistake about it.

What we have discussed here differs completely from traditional Shin Buddhist doctrinal interpretations, which simply understand Amida Buddha in a dualistic way. They

The Shin Buddhist Path

claim that Amida Buddha attained Buddhahood by himself long ago and now calls out to us from the Pure Land, "Come here! Come here!" If we grasp the Pure Land teaching in this dualistic manner, it would no longer be Buddhism. This kind of approach is often seen in Western culture. Science, for instance, was born out of such a dualistic perspective. The reason that science did not arise in the East is that such a dualistic way of seeing things was not fully developed there.

As we look out into the twenty-first century, we see a highly advanced scientific culture that is replete with all kinds of contradictions and problems. A dark shadow now hangs over the very future of our planet and the human race. At such a moment, I believe that an Eastern, non-dualistic system of thought, which is based on a standpoint quite different from Western science, can surely point humanity in a new direction toward the future. I also believe that the logical structure of Pure Land thought, which takes the standpoint of non-duality even while it accommodates dualistic expressions, can perform a vital role in mediating between the dualistic ideas of Western culture and the non-dualistic ideas of Eastern culture.

Pure Land Buddhism, I feel, can be particularly important in facilitating interchange between the spiritual cultures and ideas of the West and those of the East. I think that it can aid in the meaningful formation of a new

Western spiritual culture. In a sense, Zen Buddhism has received a great amount of attention from the dualistic Western culture, and it has been able to attract great interest because of its non-dualistic stance. However, if Zen thought is not thoroughly understood and if one does not plunge into its considerable depths, then real Zen may never come to be realized. On that point, it seems to me that in Pure Land Buddhist thought, the treatment of dualistic ideas shares much in common with Western spiritual culture, especially Christianity. Thus, it should be able to help bring about mutual understanding and fruitful results to dialogue and interchange between the East and the West.

The Pure Land Buddhist Path

Hearing the Name and Seeing the Buddha

Let us now consider the Pure Land Buddhist path of realizing true *shinjin*, the experience of awakening. As we have already seen, the Pure Land teaching is based on two standpoints. The first comprehends Amida Buddha as a word: the Name "Namu Amida Butsu." The second grasps Amida Buddha as form: the Buddha-body.

In the first case, since the Name "Namu Amida Butsu" is a word, our hearing that Name bears important implications for realizing *shinjin*, the experience of awakening. It represents a crucial opportunity to encounter Amida Buddha. In other words, this is the path of attaining Buddhahood through hearing the Name. In the second case, where Amida Buddha is represented as form, the experience of awakening comes about when one visualizes the Buddha-body. This path to enlightenment is the path of seeing the Buddha.

Of course, on the paths of hearing the Name and seeing the Buddha, "hearing" and "seeing" are not simply acts in the ordinary, worldly sense. "Hearing" as used here means that we make the ears of our minds lucid, calm, and focused, so that through the "mind's ears" we will be able to hear the Name of the Buddha; we are able to hear the calling voice of the Buddha. In the same manner, "seeing" means that we open the eyes of our minds, and with the "mind's eyes" we are able to visualize the image of Amida Buddha. These are the two kinds of paths of practice leading to enlightenment in Pure Land Buddhism.

A question must now be raised. Which path—the path of hearing the Buddha's Name or the path of seeing the Buddha-body—is the central Pure Land path? In order to answer this question, we must once again consider the origin of the Pure Land teachings. As we saw earlier, the teaching of Amida Buddha was originally expounded for the sake of the common masses made up of lay householders. In particular, it was revealed to be a path upon which those living in the lowest levels of society, those unable to perform worthy acts but who instead foolishly commit karmic evil, and those whom Shinran would later call "evil persons," could learn the Buddha-dharma and realize the experience of awakening.

The path of visualizing the Buddha was a higher grade of path, on which the practitioner was required to meditate continuously in order to purify and settle his mind. This path of practice was extremely difficult for the ordinary masses to perform, and so it was unsuitable for such ordinary beings or evil persons. In contrast, the path of earnestly hearing the Name of Amida Buddha was an extremely easy path, which anyone could perform. Hence, this path of hearing the Name was selected and revealed to be the path of practice formed by Amida Buddha's Primal Vow, which is the Buddha's aspiration to make all persons equally realize awakening and attain Buddhahood. We can conclude, therefore, that the central Pure Land Buddhist path of practice is the path of hearing the Name.

Saying the Name and Hearing the Name

The most precise and thorough explanation of this path of hearing the Name can be found in the *Larger Sutra of Immeasurable Life*. Among the Primal Vows of Amida Buddha, which the sutra expounds, the Eighteenth Vow establishes the path upon which ordinary beings and evil persons can attain Buddhahood.

> All beings! If you hear Amida Buddha's Name—that calling voice—with a true mind (sincere mind), entrusting (mind of entrusting) and wishing to be born in the Pure Land (desire for birth), and say the *nembutsu* throughout your lives, then, no matter how serious your karmic evil may be, I will enable all of you to realize birth in the Pure Land and attain Buddhahood. If this should not be fulfilled, I will not realize the enlightenment of the Buddha.[4]

This Vow begins by declaring that hearing the Buddha's Name is the path to Buddhahood. It then states that the path also involves saying the Buddha's Name and having the threefold mind of *shinjin*. We will now consider the relationship between hearing the Name, saying the Name, and realizing *shinjin*, as they pertain to Amida Buddha's Name.

The first person to clearly address this issue was Nāgārjuna of India. Born just as the Pure Land teaching was being formed, he took refuge in that teaching and brought about a deeper understanding of it. Nāgārjuna's understanding of the Pure Land teaching led him to consider the practice of hearing the Buddha's Name in this way: as the practitioner worships and thinks on Amida Buddha, and recites the Buddha's Name, he "hears" that Buddha's calling voice. That is what is meant by hearing the Name. For Nāgārjuna, hearing the Name—the Buddhist path of realizing the experience of awakening and encountering Amida Buddha through the Buddha's Name—had to be based on one's actions performed in the three modes of action; that is, the practitioner would have to engage in devoted worship (bodily action), mindfulness (mental action), and recitation of the Buddha's Name (verbal action). As a result, as Pure Land Buddhism developed, the path of hearing the Name was taken to involve the acts of worship, mindfulness, and recitation. This approach, and in particular the exclusive practice of saying the Name, gained wide acceptance by Pure Land Buddhists in China and Japan.

Shinran, however, returned this path of saying the Name back to the original standpoint of the *Larger Sutra of Immeasurable Life*. His approach was this: As we say the *nembutsu*, we hear the Buddha naming itself, the calling voice of the Buddha. And at the instant that the Buddha's calling voice comes to us to be heard, we realize *shinjin*, the experience of awakening. In other words, the Eighteenth Vow forms the path of saying the Name, hearing the Name, and realizing *shinjin*. Shinran clarified the meaning of hearing the Name by returning to the path of practice set

The Shin Buddhist Path

out in that Vow.

In the next section, we will focus on this teaching of Shinran. However, before we do, I would like to make a small comment here regarding propagation or preaching in American Shin Buddhist temples.

In Sunday Dharma School, it seems as though children are presented with the teachings of Gautama Buddha and are taught that they should do a variety of good acts. For instance, they are told to practice the six paramita or follow the eightfold noble path. However, when those children become adults and go to worship services at Shin Buddhist temples, it is explained to them that such practices (roots of good) all constitute acts of self-power. As such, they are told, these actions are wrong and should not be performed. This completely contradicts what they were taught as children. I have heard that resident ministers are quite troubled by this situation, and I must say that this kind of interpretation of the Shin Buddhist path of practice is completely mistaken.

The basic teaching of Buddhism is the instruction, presented by Gautama Buddha, that one should practice and amass all kinds of roots of good. This teaching, however, gradually intensified and became more sweeping in its application. As a result, there were few among the common people living at the base of society who could cultivate roots of good. Those persons, as well as evil persons who committed many acts of karmic evil, were therefore urged to perform the practices of hearing the Name and saying the Name, which were much easier to carry out.

In other words, the Pure Land Buddhist path in effect consolidates the various and sundry practices into one act that is easy to perform. Therefore, the Pure Land Buddhist path of hearing the Name and saying the Name is consistent in its adoption of the basic structure of the original Buddhist path: through the cultivation of various roots of good, one realizes the experience of awakening. It appears that some persons are trying to explain the Pure Land path of practice without really understanding it. This situation can be seen today among Shin Buddhists in Japan, and apparently in America as well.

Path of Teaching, Practice, and Realization

Today, the original teachings of Gautama Buddha are largely compiled in the Pali scriptural texts. A perusal of them reveals that the structure of the path leading to the experience of awakening is based for the most part on three kinds of virtue: belief, practice, and wisdom.

Belief means that one learns the teachings correctly and believes in them with confidence. Practice refers to performing the actions and practices that are stipulated in those teachings. Wisdom refers to awakening, which is the ultimate goal of the Buddhist path of practice. This means that, by believing in the teachings and single-heartedly performing the practices set forth in them, one will be able to reach the sphere of wisdom, or the experience of awakening, without fail. This is the Buddhist path of belief, practice, and wisdom, which was taught in original Buddhism. Later forms of Buddhism each emphasized their own varieties of paths. But, no matter what form of Buddhism they might have taken, they all prescribed nothing other than some version of the path of belief, practice, and wisdom.

Shinran described the Shin Buddhist path in terms of a threefold structure of teaching, practice, and realization. Here, teaching means that one entrusts deeply in the teachings that one has chosen. Practice refers to those karmic actions that are prescribed in those teachings. Realization signifies awakening; it is an expression of wisdom. This threefold structure—teaching, practice, and realization—represented, in effect, Shinran's adoption of the path of belief, practice, and wisdom of original Buddhism. In Chinese Buddhism that original path was reinterpreted to be teaching, practice, and realization, and that structure was later transmitted to Japan. The doctrine of the Tendai school of Buddhism, which Shinran studied as a young monk on Mt. Hiei, also clarified the path for attaining Buddhahood through the threefold concept of teaching, practice, and realization. We know that this was not the case just for Shinran alone. Both Dōgen (1200-1253) and Nichiren (1222-1282) had also studied the Buddhist teachings on Mt. Hiei during their early years, and both described the same threefold structure of their own Buddhist paths. It could be said that virtually every school of Buddhism expounded this path of teaching, practice, and realization, which in turn represented a complete adoption of the original Buddhist path of belief, practice, and wisdom.

The Shin Buddhist way revealed by Shinran was also the path of believing deeply in the teachings, performing the practices prescribed in those teachings, and attaining realization, which is the experience of awakening. What does that path involve, concretely? Based on the teaching of the *Larger Sutra of Immeasurable Life*, which is a Mahayana Buddhist scripture, we perform the practices of hearing the Name and saying the Name, which that sutra sets forth. As a result of that, we soon realize the experience of awakening, which is the goal of the Buddhist path. Eventually on this path we realize birth in the Pure Land and attain the enlightenment of the Buddha. This is the reason that Shinran entitled his major work *A Collection of Passages Revealing the True Teaching, Practice, and Realization of the Pure Land Way*.[5] The distinguishing feature of Shinran's teaching of Shin Buddhism lies in the path of hearing the Name and saying the Name, a path of practice based on the Name of Amida Buddha. The practices provided on this path can be performed easily by evil persons who cannot cultivate roots of good, but instead only commit a variety of acts of karmic evil.

The Shin Buddhist Path

The Path that Shinran Walked

We can now take a more detailed look at the Shin Buddhist path of attaining Buddhahood, which was established by Shinran.

The central practice of the Pure Land Buddhist path, as transmitted from India to China and Japan, was basically to hear the Name of Amida Buddha while reciting that Buddha's Name. In Indian and Chinese Pure Land Buddhism, it was also taught that one must say the Name while cultivating roots of good, that is, while performing various other practices such as worship, mindfulness, and so

The Shin Buddhist Path

on. Over time there was a gradual refinement of that doctrine. In Japan it finally reached Hōnen (1133-1212), who taught that all roots of good other than saying the Name are absolutely unnecessary; the sole practice of reciting the *nembutsu* is sufficient in itself. Through his encounter with Hōnen, Shinran was able to learn this new Pure Land teaching, and then make it even more far-reaching and deeply personal.

Constant Practice of the *Nembutsu*

Let us discuss the practice of saying of the *nembutsu* on the path of Buddhahood and the meaning of "Namu Amida Butsu" in Shinran's thought.

"*Namu*" is a Japanese transliteration of the original Indian words "*namo*" or "*namas*," which are expressions of taking refuge. Hence, saying "Namu Amida Butsu" is the easiest of practices, for that simple act of taking refuge in Amida Buddha comprises both our aspiration and practice on the path to Buddhahood.

In Japanese Pure Land Buddhism prior to Shinran, recitation of the Name took the form of the "constant practice of the *nembutsu*," a regimen of concentrated practice in which one was required to recite the Name exclusively and constantly at a specified place for a fixed period of time. It was believed that if one performed the "constant practice of the *nembutsu*" one would realize the experience of awakening without fail. This was the fundamental path of practice in the Pure Land teachings, as it was transmitted from China to Japan.

Initially, it was possible to engage in the concentrated "constant practice of the *nembutsu*" at various locations within Japan. On Mt. Hiei, where Shinran labored in religious practices for twenty years during his youth, there was a hall named the "hall of constant practice." That practice hall still exists even today. Originally there were many such halls on Mt. IIiei, but only that one remains. In the very center of that hall, which is roughly nine meters square, is enshrined an image of Amida Buddha. It is there that the "constant practice of the *nembutsu*," also known as the "constant practice *samādhi*," is performed.

The "constant practice *samādhi*" is an extremely intense practice. Upon entering the hall, the practitioner recites the *nembutsu* while walking in a clockwise direction around and around the circumference of the Amida Buddha image, practicing continuously day and night, with absolutely no rest, for ninety days. Thus, "constant" means that one does not take a break throughout the day or night. "Practice" refers to the acts of walking and reciting the *nembutsu*. "*Samādhi*" is the experience of fixing one's mind and visualizing the Buddha, and thereby encountering the Buddha. The practitioner is allowed to eat three times a day, but the food is brought into the hall and one must eat standing up. There is a toilet next to the hall. The practitioner, however, is absolutely prohibited from resting in a prone position. Simply put, he must continue to walk around the interior of the hall, while fervently reciting the *nembutsu*, throughout the day and night for ninety days. This is the kind of extremely intense practice of reciting the Name that has existed on Mt. Hiei. It is believed that during his younger days, Shinran also practiced in the hall of constant practice.

Some time ago, I had the opportunity to meet a Tendai Buddhist priest from Mt. Hiei, who had performed this strenuous "constant practice *samādhi*," and to hear him speak about what it was like. He said that in ancient times a great number of priests engaged in this practice. However, since the beginning of the Meiji period, no one performed it for well over one hundred years. According to the records of old, many of those who undertook the practice became sick and died, or went mad midway through it.

According to the priest, about ten days into the practice, both his legs became enormously swollen, causing him so much pain that it felt as though he was walking on top of needles. The continuous recitation of the *nembutsu* made his throat grow parched, and after a while his voice disappeared. Both his energy and stamina waned. His distress was overwhelming and he felt that if things were to continue on in this way, he would surely die. He thought about quitting at that point, but since he had undertaken the practice in the face of opposition of many people, he felt that he could not very well quit. He also considered running away during the practice. However, he then thought about the vastness of Mt. Hiei and about how sad it would be if he were to escape into the mountains and die there, with his body left undiscovered.

With this kind of turmoil playing itself out over and over again in his mind, he continued to walk around the hall, reciting the *nembutsu*. Before long, he became aware that he was breathing, saying the *nembutsu*, and walking in fine rhythm, and that he had become able to walk quite comfortably. I do not quite understand how it happened, but he stated that as he placed one foot ahead of the other, step by step, the motion of his walking, the inhaling and exhaling of his breath, and his recitation of the *nembutsu*, all fell smoothly into a wonderful rhythm, and he was soon able to walk quite easily.

In any event, he performed this difficult practice for ninety days in that manner. The priest also explained that, as he performed this practice, his mind gradually became quite clear, and he was able to visualize beautiful flower gardens and encounter the Buddha many times. This was the kind of deeply religious and mystical experience that he was able to realize. Furthermore, he had the experience of walking across a river of water. His comment was, "I have heard that in the teachings of Shin Buddhism there is the parable of crossing over a river of fire and water in order to go to the Pure Land, isn't there?"

Living the *Nembutsu*

After descending Mt. Hiei, Shinran met Hōnen and learned of another practice of saying the *nembutsu* that differed from the "constant practice of the *nembutsu*." In this new practice one could say the *nembutsu* freely in the midst of everyday life. One could say the Name throughout one's entire life, anytime and anywhere, without having to set off a specific place or a fixed period of time. On this path, when one continued to say the *nembutsu* in the midst of one's everyday life—whether busily engaged in any kind of occupation, or whether awake or asleep in one's home—one would eventually be able to experience awakening and encounter the Buddha in the same manner as a renunciant monk. In contrast to the constant practice of the *nembutsu* like the "constant practice *samādhi*" on Mt. Hiei that we saw earlier, this practice might accurately be referred to as the "*nembutsu* of everyday life." Shinran later married and carried on the lifestyle of a householder, and he continued to say the *nembutsu* as his exclusive practice every day.

Hence, it might be said that he came to walk this path of the "*nembutsu* of everyday life."

Shinran founded this new *nembutsu* path, one that could be lived by lay householders, based on what he had learned from his teacher Hōnen. It was D. T. Suzuki (1870-1966) who translated this *nembutsu* into English as "living." I think that this is a marvelous and apt translation, and so I have chosen to call this the path of "living the *nembutsu*." This is what the "*nembutsu* of everyday life" means: within the circumstances of an everyday life covered with the stains of the secular world, we think on the Buddha and say the *nembutsu* in whatever condition—whether laughing or crying, angry, or happy—that we may find ourselves in.

Through this *nembutsu* practiced every day of our lives, a path opens up before us, and on that path we are able to realize the experience of true awakening and attain Buddhahood. This is the path that Shinran experienced and has revealed to us. The Pure Land teaching of Amida Buddha is a form of Buddhism for "evil persons," the common masses who live at the base of society, who have scant ability to practice good acts, and who instead commit all sorts of karmic evil. This Pure Land teaching becomes most vividly revealed here in Shinran's assertion that it is the evil person who in fact attains Buddhahood.

Shin Buddhism reveals a path of practice in which one can actually experience *shinjin* or awakening, and attain

Buddhahood through this kind of "*nembutsu* of everyday life."

The *Nembutsu* of "Choice"

The *Nembutsu* Alone Is True and Real

Let us consider a little more the content of the Shin Buddhist practice of the "*nembutsu* of everyday life," that is, the recitation of the *nembutsu* as "living," as taught to us by Shinran.

More than anything else, the *nembutsu* of everyday life must be a "*nembutsu* of choice." Like Shinran before us, we must choose the *nembutsu* as the practice of our lives, risking our own subjectivity. This is the quintessence of the *nembutsu* that was expounded by Hōnen and taught by Shinran. For instance, at the end of *A Record in Lament of Divergences* (*Tannishō*) are these famous words,

> But with a foolish being full of blind passions, in this fleeting world—this burning house—all matters without exception are empty and false, totally without truth and sincerity. The nembutsu alone is true and real.[6]

Here the words "the *nembutsu* alone" mean that we

choose one thing alone: the *nembutsu*. We say the *nembutsu* in the midst of all of the circumstances of everyday life. What is more important, however, is that as we say the *nembutsu*, we "choose to accept" it as the only thing that is true and real, and we "choose to reject" everything else as being empty and false, full of lies and deceit.

In our ordinary lives, we always think that our parents or children, or our husbands or wives, are our most important treasures. Or, we feel that fortune, fame, and social status are the most important values that we have. Thus we busy ourselves throughout our daily lives, trying hard either to obtain such values or to protect them. However, are these really the most important things in our lives? Is it not true that all of these treasures and values will eventually fade away and crumble? Not one of them, we come to learn, is ultimately true and real. Every single one of them is actually "empty and false."

How deeply will we come to know this truth of the way things actually are? Also, to what extent will we be able to "de-absolutize" the worldly values that we so desperately seek after? Will we be able to choose to abandon them? Only if we choose to reject all worldly values—if we recognize that their worth is relative to something else and that they are lacking in absolute truth—can we choose to understand that "the *nembutsu* alone is true and real."

The *nembutsu*, which Shinran teaches us, is the

nembutsu that we say in our daily lives, as we realize keenly and deeply that no worldly values are either thoroughgoing or true. Or, stated conversely, as we say the *nembutsu*, we come to realize that all worldly values are false. And, based upon that realization, we come to comprehend even more that the *nembutsu* alone is true. This is what it means to "live" the *nembutsu*. Thus, the *nembutsu*, as taught to us by Shinran, is the "*nembutsu* of choice."

Nembutsu as "Living"

Whenever one of my graduating students has asked me to write some parting words, it has been my custom to write the following: "Know that all the events of this world—whatever they may be, whenever they may be—are conditions that support the *nembutsu*." These words are sort of my motto. They are words that I always write, not because I necessarily live by them, but in a sense because they are cautionary words for me. The words urge me to say the *nembutsu* knowing that, no matter how sad an event may be or how angry I may become over some incident, everything that happens in my life works its way "toward" me so that I will not forget the *nembutsu*, or so that I will say the *nembutsu* many times or say it even just once. Because that is so, I will always be able to overcome any sadness or suffering, and a new way will open up within my life. In my understanding, this path is the *"nembutsu* of everyday life"—the *nembutsu* as "living"—that Shinran teaches us.

When I speak about such things to regular temple members, I usually phrase it in this way: the *nembutsu* is the single treasure that we can bring along with us when we die. No matter how much fame, status, fortune, or even love that we may possess in life, we will not be able to bring any of them with us when we die. We must leave everything behind. No matter how loving of a parent or spouse we may be, since we are alone at our birth, we will also be alone at our death. Each one of us must die alone. Yet, when each one of us dies alone, bringing along nothing else with us, there will still be one single treasure that we will surely have: the *nembutsu*. This is what I always tell people.

A number of years ago, I went to pay a visit to an elderly member of my home temple who was dying of cancer of the larynx. He had been going to the temple quite often for a very long time, and so, as I sat beside his bed, I felt that I could say to him, "In the end, all that's left is the *nembutsu*."

The old man responded with a deep, knowing nod, and said only, "Thank you. Thank you." The next day, he died.

Another temple member passed away while I was in Kyoto and I was unable to see him. But he left a letter, which he had dictated and addressed to me. He said the same thing: "I am not worried, for I am dying with the *nembutsu*. Thank you." To live, all the while humbly saying the *nembutsu*, then to die having the treasure of that *nembutsu*—that is the fundamental way of life and death for the Shin Buddhist. I am joyful as I think about all those people in my life who have gone before me, the many *nembutsu* followers who have walked the path ahead of me.

Continuous Practice of the *Nembutsu* Every Day

Shinran also spoke vigorously about the continuation of the practice of the *nembutsu*, urging people to say the *nembutsu* continuously each and every day. For instance, he states with great intensity,

> Those who deeply entrust themselves
> To Amida's Vow of great compassion
> Should all say Namu-amida-butsu constantly
> Whether they are waking or sleeping.[7]

Shinran is urging us to say the *nembutsu* in any situation, whether asleep or awake, whether in our cars or in our beds, whether happy or sad, or even when we have nothing else at all. We should consider any event that occurs in our lives to be a condition that supports the *nembutsu* and say the Name with that thought in mind. That would truly be a "*nembutsu* of everyday life," because the *nembutsu* would in reality become everyday life for each one of us. The Shin Buddhist path—the true path to the attainment of Buddhahood—can be found in our continued calling of the Buddha's Name each and every day of our lives.

When I was a child, whenever any temple had a Dharma-gathering, all of the members would say the *nembutsu* as they listened to the minister's sermon. During the breaks between talks, all in attendance would say the *nembutsu* in unison. As a result, one could hear a pattern of alternating rhythm between the words of the minister giving the sermon and the voices of the members calling out the *nembutsu*. Today in Japan, however, that custom has gradually disappeared and the voices of the *nembutsu* can no longer be heard. I would like to be able to hear those voices of the *nembutsu* one more time.

Those voices were heard in America as well. Some twenty years ago I had the chance to visit the University of Washington in Seattle. At that time in Seattle there was an association of people who came from Hiroshima prefecture, and, since I am also from Hiroshima, they gave me a welcome party. That led to my being asked to give a talk at the Sunday worship service at the Seattle Buddhist Temple.

While I was giving my talk, something happened that surprised me greatly. As I spoke, the entire hall began

The Shin Buddhist Path

welling up with the *nembutsu*. Around three hundred people were at that temple worship service and they were all saying the *nembutsu* in unison, in response to my talk. I was deeply moved by the experience. Later, one of the members told me that they had been taught to do so by their parents. They were taught that when they went to the temple to hear a Dharma talk, they were to say the *nembutsu* while listening. It gave me great joy to know that, even though the temple members were third and fourth generation Japanese-Americans and the Japanese language was gradually being forgotten, the *nembutsu* was definitely still alive in this way.

That happened twenty years ago. I often wonder what has become of that *nembutsu* now. In any case, we can be aware of those who went before us, living their lives as they said the *nembutsu*. This is what it means to live the *nembutsu* continuously.

Nembutsu and *Shinjin*

Nembutsu History

Why are we able to encounter the Buddha when we say the *nembutsu*? How is it that the experience of awakening, that is, true and real *shinjin*, comes about through saying the *nembutsu*? These questions become extremely important, especially when we talk about transmitting and hearing the teachings.

First, those who have said the *nembutsu* every day and have attained the experience of awakening have walked (and are walking) on the path before us. A "*nembutsu* history" exists in the footprints of those *nembutsu* followers. This is an unquestionable fact. I have known many such *nembutsu* followers in America. In Japan as well, of course, this history has continued unbroken even up to this very day.

There is a history to the *nembutsu*. As we learn of the *nembutsu* of Shin Buddhism, it is very important that we first come into contact with this *nembutsu* history. Concretely, this history has a human character. It involves human life: a person who has attained the experience of awakening by saying the *nembutsu* or a person who says the *nembutsu* while walking ahead of us toward the Pure Land. Of course, it may also consist of the life stories or the words left by those who have already passed away. In any case, it is important that we encounter this history in the concrete reality of a human personality.

In the Meiji period there lived a Shin Buddhist priest by the name of Shichiri Gōjun (1835-1900). Here is one of his sayings.

Wandering aimlessly over train tracks will not allow

us to board the train. If we want to try to reach our destination, we should go to the train station. There we should buy a ticket and board the train.

This means that it does not matter how much we may learn about Buddhist theory and doctrine. If we do not encounter a real human personality, it will all amount to nothing. Shichiri compares this human personality to a train station. Only by going to the station—by encountering a human personality and coming into contact with a definite *nembutsu* history—will we finally be able to reach our destination. I think that this is a truly splendid illustration of the *nembutsu* history.

Psychology of the *Nembutsu*

Next, let us consider why we are able to realize the expcrience of awakening when we say the *nembutsu*, that is, when we call the Buddha's Name. The answer lies in the structure of the act of saying the *nembutsu* itself.

When we earnestly call the Buddha's Name with a fullness of heart while listening to the dharma, our lives gradually become directed toward the Buddha. However, as our recitation of the *nembutsu* deepens, there is an eventual reversal in the direction of that *nembutsu*. When we say the *nembutsu*, we are directing ourselves toward the Buddha as we call out the Buddha's Name and think on the Buddha. However, at the same time, we also awaken to a movement in the opposite direction. That is, we hear the voice of the Buddha that is directing itself to us, as it names itself and calls out to us. Here, a transcendent religious experience takes place, which we awaken to at the deepest level of our consciousness.

This experience takes place as an inevitable result of our religious and psychological functioning as human beings. For Shinran, it also arises as the necessary consequence of Amida Buddha's Primal Vow. That is to say, the fundamental structure of the experience of awakening is necessarily identical to that of saying the *nembutsu*. As I have mentioned earlier, this was how Shinran explained the logical structure of saying the *nembutsu*: our act of saying the *nembutsu* is our own act, which comprises both aspiration and practice. That is, we say "Namu" and take refuge in "Amida Butsu." (*Namu Amida Butsu*= "I return to the life of the Buddha.") However, Shinran also understood that the practice of saying the *nembutsu* is the Buddha's calling voice, which comprises aspiration and practice, in the sense that "Amida Butsu" performs the act of "Namu" and takes refuge in us. (*Namu Amida Butsu*= "The Buddha's command that calls out to me to return to the Buddha.") This is what saying the *nembutsu* means.

From our perspective, that is, from the viewpoint of the psychology of the *nembutsu*, the practice of saying the *nembutsu* enables us to "de-absolutize" and unconditionally reject all worldly views. Each of us busies himself or herself by taking a wife or taking a husband, bearing children, or seeking fame and fortune. However, when our lives are occupied with learning the dharma and saying the *nembutsu*, all of these things begin to fade away before long. Eventually, all will be taken from our hands. When we die, we cannot bring any of them with us; we must leave all of them behind. Hence, we come to an ever deepening realization that all such things are empty and false.

When the current state of our own existence is seen in this way and it is gradually "de-absolutized" and rejected, then our own selves become emptied. It is then, inevitably, that something comes to be heard. Normally, we are always trying to cram ourselves full of things. We are constantly filling ourselves up with self-attachment and ego, and so we are unable to see or hear anything truly. However, when our selves gradually become emptied, then the eyes of our minds will open and we will finally be able to see things. The ears of our minds will become clear and we will be able to hear things for the first time. And we are able to hear other persons' voices of distress and pain as well.

When we come to know keenly and fully that the current state of our existence is false and empty, then we will become able to hear what we had not been able to hear up until now. We will be able to see what up until now we had not been able to see. Within this structure, finally, we become able to hear the voice of the Buddha within the *nembutsu*. This is how saying the *nembutsu* works in Shin Buddhism.

An identical structure can be found for awakening or enlightenment in Gautama Buddha's teaching. There, enlightenment is referred to as "emancipation." Emancipation means to "remove" or "cast off." That is, one removes or casts off one's old skin. The self is extinguished and gradually becomes empty. Further, the Buddhist teaching refers to the attainment of enlightenment as "becoming Buddha." To attain Buddhahood is to "become." One realizes growth and becomes a new self. In Buddhism awakening or enlightenment has this kind of dual structure of "casting off" and "becoming."

Awakening through saying the *nembutsu* also has exactly the same kind of structure. As our old selves become emptied, new selves become fully matured. As our selves become emptied, something new comes to be heard or seen. In the end, the voice of the Buddha that is calling to us comes to be heard, or perceived, in the ears of our minds. Shinran referred to this "structure of reversal" when he stated that to say the Name is to hear the Name, and to hear the Name is to say the Name.

The Shin Buddhist Path

Here is an illustration. When we were children, we would eagerly called out the names of our parents by saying "Mom!" or "Dad!" We would call out "Mom!" to our mothers and they would answer "Yes!" to us. However, if we really think about this, it was because we received our mothers' love that we called out to them. If we had not received our mothers' love, we would never have done so. When we were infants, how often did we all call out the names of our parents? It is because we continued to call out to them constantly that, now, we are aware that our parents' love was already there before we called out their names. We know that, in effect, we were being called by our parents. We realize that our calling of our parents' names is nothing more than an echo of our parents' voices calling to us.

As we continue to practice the *nembutsu* as "living" within our ordinary lives—saying the *nembutsu* as we continue to direct our lives toward the Buddha and being ever mindful of the Buddha—inevitably, this religious experience of reversal will eventually come about. An experience of awakening ("Ah! That's what it was! That's how it is!") will take place. Awakening means that we experience a recollection deeply in our hearts and realize the truth of something long forgotten (*omoiataru*) and that we understand something so deeply that we are convinced of its reality beyond any doubt (*fu ni ochiru*). As I mentioned earlier, when a child calls out "Mom!" to its mother, at a deeper level, the mother is calling out to her child. The mother's heart echoes, or reverberates, within her child's heart, and therefore the child calls out "Mom!" This activity takes place in both directions. The child's calling out "Mom!" to the parent intersects with the parent's love for the child.

As we continue to call out the Name of the Buddha ("Namu Amida Butsu! Namu Amida Butsu!") our selves become emptied and we experience deeply the truth of something long forgotten—that our saying of the Name, in which we call out to the Buddha, is itself the Buddha's calling out to us. When this occurs, it is called the experience of awakening. This is *shinjin*, which comes to be realized through saying the *nembutsu*. It represents ultimate religious experience in Shin Buddhism.

Shinran said that the act of saying the *nembutsu*, in which we call out the Name of the Buddha, will inevitably reverse its direction and become the act of hearing of the Name, wherein the Buddha calls out to us. As we say the Name it is important that we experience deeply the truth that it is the voice of the Buddha calling out to us. Shinran further said that truly hearing the Name is to realize *shinjin*. Therefore, he stated that truly saying the Name and true *shinjin* are identical.

However, strictly speaking, Shinran also said that,

The Shin Buddhist Path

although *shinjin* is identical with saying the *nembutsu*, there are cases when saying the *nembutsu* is not necessarily identical with *shinjin*. That is to say, a unidirectional *nembutsu*, in which we say the *nembutsu* to the Buddha but do not hear the *nembutsu* as the voice of the Buddha calling out to us from the opposite direction, is not a true *nembutsu*. Such a *nembutsu* would not be identical with *shinjin*. However, truly saying the *nembutsu* necessarily involves a real religious experience—a profound experiencing of the truth of something long forgotten—in which what has been recited is heard coming from the opposite direction.

Shinran referred to this ultimate religious experience as "*shinjin*." He then taught us to realize this experience of awakening, this religious experience of *shinjin*, as we say the *nembutsu*. In that sense, truly saying the *nembutsu* signifies, in and of itself, hearing the Name and *shinjin*. Hence, in Shinran's thought, the relationship between saying the *nembutsu*, hearing the Name, and realizing *shinjin* is indeed one of mutual identity.

Nembutsu and *Shinjin*

There is also an aspect to the relationship between the *nembutsu* and *shinjin* wherein it can be said that the life of saying the *nembutsu* is a process that leads us along a path to the realization of *shinjin* as the ultimate religious experience. At the same time, however, when this practice of the *nembutsu* becomes the true *nembutsu*, it can also be said that there is no *shinjin* apart from that *nembutsu*. In that sense, the true *nembutsu* is never separate from the ultimate goal. As we earnestly say the *nembutsu*, in a process whereby it becomes our very life, we come to realize *shinjin* and encounter the Buddha. However, at the same time, *shinjin*, or our encounter with the Buddha, cannot exist apart from the *nembutsu* that we recite each and every day of our lives. Thus, the *nembutsu* is not just a mere process or expedient means. The true *nembutsu* is *shinjin*, in and of itself. *Shinjin* also exists together with that *nembutsu*. Hence, Shinran states,

> [T]here is no shinjin separate from nembutsu; this is the teaching I have received. You should know further that there can be no nembutsu separate from shinjin.[8]

The *nembutsu* is identical with *shinjin*; *shinjin* is identical with the *nembutsu*. The *nembutsu* and *shinjin* are inseparable and non-dual. Since in Shinran's thought the *nembutsu* is a practice, the identity of the *nembutsu* and *shinjin* can also be described as the non-duality of practice and *shinjin*.

In Zen thought, a form of Buddhism for renunciant monks, *Dōgen* makes the same assertion when he states

The Shin Buddhist Path

"practice is equivalent to enlightenment." Here, "practice" refers to seated meditation (*zazen*), which represents a process on the path to Buddhahood. "Enlightenment" is the ultimate goal of that path. "Equivalent" refers to oneness or non-discrimination. In *Dōgen*'s thought, sitting is in itself enlightenment. Aside from enlightenment there is no sitting; there is no enlightenment apart from sitting. Sitting and enlightenment are non-dual.

Shinran's path of practicing the *nembutsu* has the same fundamental logic. In one sense, the *nembutsu* and *shinjin* are separate matters. However, in the true practice of the *nembutsu*, the *nembutsu* is identical with *shinjin*, and *shinjin* is identical with the *nembutsu*. Practice and *shinjin* are one and the same. They are non-dual. We must become persons who are able to say this kind of *nembutsu*. *Dōgen*'s path of seated meditation is a form of Buddhism for renunciant monks, and it is necessary to practice it at a specific place and for a fixed time, away from the secular world. For that reason, it can be done only by a limited number of persons having the ability to do so. However, the path of the *nembutsu*, which Shinran teaches us, can take place in the midst of the secular world in any kind of lifestyle. When we live by earnestly saying the *nembutsu* as "living" and concentrate our minds on the Buddha—dharma in the midst of this lay householder's life, we will be able to attain the same realm of ultimate awakening.

D. T. Suzuki said that the ultimate experience of enlightenment of a Zen master, realized after the fulfillment of profound practices, and the awakening experienced by humble persons of *shinjin* (*myōkōnin*) in the Shin Buddhist tradition, who say the *nembutsu* while engaged in any variety of occupations in the very midst of secular life, are exactly the same. Our discussion here has shown the basis for Suzuki's assertion.

NOTES

1 Bukkyō Dendō Kyōkai, *The Teachings of the Buddha*, (Tokyo: Kōsaido, 1998), 18.
2 "On Jinen Hōni," see Shin Buddhism Translation Series, *The Collected Works of Shinran*, Vol. I (hereinafter CWS), (Kyoto: Jōdo Shinshū Hongwanji-ha, 1997), 427-428.
3 From the Eighteenth Vow of the *Larger Sutra*, cited in CWS, 80.
4 This rephrasing of the Eighteenth Vow and the passage on the fulfillment of the Eighteenth Vow has been done to capture the essential purport of the Vow.
5 This is the English title of Shinran's major work, *Ken Shinjitsu Kyōgyōshō Monrui*, as rendered by the Shin Buddhist Translation Center.
6 *A Record in Lament of Divergences* (*Tannishō*), in CWS, 679.
7 *Hymns of the Dharma-Ages* (*Shōzōmatsu Wasan*), in CWS,

411.

8   *Lamp for the Latter Ages* (*Mattōshō*), in CWS, 538.

Part Two

Shinjin

Chapter One

The Idea of *Shin* in Buddhism

General Notions of *Shin*

We will now consider the meaning of *shinjin* in Shin Buddhism. Please understand that my approach to *shinjin* is somewhat different from the interpretations found in traditional doctrinal studies. I believe, however, that what I am about to present reflects the true, inner reality of *shinjin*, as it was taught to us by Shinran.

When I last visited Berkeley twenty years ago, I participated in many study sessions with Shin Buddhist ministers in America. At that time, the following discussion took place. It seems that at Buddhist temples the Japanese word "*shin*" (信)[1] was almost always translated as "faith," as in "I put my faith in Amida Buddha." One minister mentioned that he was troubled about this, for he did not know how to answer a question that had been put to him by a member. The question was this: "Christianity teaches people to have faith in God. At this temple, we are instructed to put our faith in Amida Buddha. So what is the difference between Christianity and Shin Buddhism? Is it just that we have different objects of faith?" The minister wondered how best to answer this question. At that time, I responded by saying that I had many problems with translating *shinjin* in Shin Buddhism as "faith." I mentioned that *shinjin*, as explained by Shinran, is quite different from the "faith" found in most religions. I would now like to discuss that difference.

Belief and Faith

Secular Notions of *Shin*: Belief

Before talking about the content of *shin* in Buddhism, I would like to consider other kinds of *shin*. Generally, when the word *shin* is used in the realm of human relationships, it corresponds to the English word "belief" (*shinyō* or *shinrai* in Japanese). In addition, there is a form of *shin* that generally corresponds to the notion of "faith" (*shinkō* in Japanese) in religions. In this sense, *shin* means that one places one's faith in an absolute God. I believe that there are differences between the secular notion of belief and this religious concept of faith.

Both secular belief and religious faith presume a relationship between a subject and an object. They are objective forms of *shin*, since they involve a subject that believes (or has faith) and an object which is believed (or in which one has faith). On this point, belief and faith are similar, since both involve the sense either of believing or having faith in something. However, there are differences between secular belief and religious faith. The first difference is that belief takes as its object something in the secular world, while faith takes as its object something transcendental and eternal. Secular belief is concerned with some object within this world, whereas religious faith is directed toward an object that transcends this world.

Another difference is that secular belief can occur only if one has a certain degree of proof, which would allow a person to believe. For instance, we can believe in our companion, such as a spouse or a friend, because our longstanding relationship gives us definite proof that we can trust that person. On the other hand, we are not very likely to leave a bag filled with money in the care of a person whom we have just met for the first time. That is because we do not know whether we can believe in that person or not, since we do not have any proof allowing us to trust that person. Here is another example. Most of us are willing to board airplanes or ships, even though accidents sometimes occur on both of them. This is because we know that even though many airplanes go aloft, they seldom crash, and ships almost never sink. Taking this knowledge as evidence, we board them in the belief that everything will probably be all right.

This kind of proof always involves an issue of probability. In some cases the probabilities may be extremely cruel, as when we are told that we have an illness that is likely incurable and we will be able to return to health only by the slimmest of chances. On the other hand, we might be told that we need not worry about an illness, for we will almost certainly become well again. The proof upon which we base our beliefs is really just a matter of probability. Still, we cling to any kind of evidence that will allow us to believe that everything will probably be okay. That means, however, that there will also be times when persons or things, which we had believed in, betray our trust.

In order to live as human beings in this world we have to believe in a range of people and things. Yet our world can also be a world of tears when those in whom we had believed prove untrustworthy. This is the kind of life that we human beings all live. I also believe that this is the meaning of secular *shin*, or belief.

General Religious Notions of *Shin*: Faith

In many religious forms of *shin*, by contrast, people place their faith in an absolute being or in the transcendent. Here, the object of their faith is something that is eternal and transcends this world. This is an objective kind of faith, in that it takes as its object something that is eternal and ultimate, whether we call it "God," "Buddha," or something else. Moreover, this kind of faith is completely lacking in any rational or objective proof. Does God exist or not? Do heaven and hell exist, or do they not? There is nothing that can confirm or deny any of these matters in an objective way. There is no way to prove or disprove them. For instance, God, heaven, and hell are matters that transcend the human intellect. Thus, it is impossible to prove that they exist. At the same time, it is impossible to prove that they do not exist. Such matters transcend human judgment and cognition. When, in spite of that, people still acknowledge the existence or reality of such things, they are exercising this kind of religious faith.

"We must surrender our intellect in order to have faith." "Because it makes no sense, we have to put our faith in it." "Faith is a gamble." Such expressions point to the structure in which this kind of generic, religious faith arises: by eliminating all intellectual functioning, people offer unquestioning endorsement to the object of their faith, and gamble upon something for which there can be no certainty.

Buddhist Notions of *Shin*

Shin as *Prasāda*

The nature of *shin* in Buddhism is quite different from the secular form of *shin* (belief) and the religious form of *shin* (faith).

A number of Sanskrit terms serve as the basis for the word *shin* in Buddhism. One of them is *prasāda*, which in the Pure Land sutras is used to denote entrusting (*shin-jiru* in Japanese) in Amida Buddha. This term means, among other things, "purity," "joy," and "clarity." It has been translated into Chinese as *shōjō* or *chōjō* (purity), *jōshin* (pure trust), *shingyō* (entrusting with joy), and *shinjin*.

I recall hearing this explanation from a teacher during my student days: Deep within the mountains there exists a pond. The water in that pond is perfectly clean and pure. The surface of the pond, moreover, is so calm and tranquil that it is just like a mirror. The state of the water in that pond, said my teacher, is what is meant by *prasāda*.

In the Sanskrit version of the *Larger Sutra of Immeasurable Life*, the word *prasāda-citta* appears in the passage on the Primal Vow to express entrusting in Amida Buddha. Citta means "heart and mind." That is, one's heart and mind becomes pure and one realizes joy. In Buddhism, citta also refers to fundamental human consciousness. It points to the deepest and most basic level of an individual human being's subjectivity. Stated further, it may be said that this heart and mind is identical with the life of each and every person. Therefore, *prasāda*-citta means that one's mind—one's fundamental personal subjectivity or human life—becomes pure and clear, and one realizes joy.

In the Chinese translation of the *Larger Sutra*, the Primal Vow teaches sentient beings to "entrust with joy" (*shingyō*) in Amida Buddha. *Shingyō* is a translation of *prasāda*. Since *prasāda* means that one's heart and mind becomes pure and one realizes joy, it was translated as "entrust with joy." A later passage in the *Larger Sutra* clarifies the meaning of the Primal Vow by using another phrase, "realize *shinjin* and joy" (*shinjin kangi*). This is another expression for "entrust with joy" (*shingyō*). *Shinjin* is equivalent to *shin* (entrust) and kangi is the same as *gyō* (joy). Hence, both are Chinese translations of the original term *prasāda*. We can see that entrusting in Amida Buddha refers to a state of mind, *prasāda-citta*, in which one's heart and mind become pure and serene, giving rise to great joy.

Shinjin is Non-dualistic and Subjective

I think that you can see that the Buddhist notion of *shin* means something quite different from either belief in the secular sense or faith in the generic religious sense.

The first difference between them is that *shinjin* in Shinran's teaching of Shin Buddhism does not refer to a dualistic frame of mind in which we take something as the object of our belief or faith. *Prasāda*, or *shinjin*, signifies a state in which our own hearts and minds become pure, and we attain great joy. This form of *shin* is completely non-dualistic and subjective in nature. It does not imply that we must do something *vis-à-vis* some object.

Shinjin as the Experience of Awakening

The second difference between *shin* and the notions of secular belief and religious faith is that the realm of *prasāda*, or *shinjin*, transcends this secular world. Expressing this in terms of Buddhist doctrine, *shinjin* is equivalent to the state of *samādhi* in which one visualizes the Buddha. It points to the experience of awakening, whereby one directly encounters the Buddha. In the words of Shinran, *shinjin* is the experience in which one comes to hear the calling voice of the Buddha.

Nāgārjuna writes about Amida Buddha in his text *The*

Shinjin

Commentary on the Ten Bodhisattva Stages. Since no original Indian text exists, we can only rely upon the Chinese translation. In his "Chapter on Easy Practice" of this text, he states,

> But for those whose shinjin is pure,
> The flower opens, and immediately they see the Buddha.[2]

I believe that this passage also describes the realm of samādhi, or visualizing the Buddha, which is expressed as prasāda. Shinran cites this passage within his own works as well.

Shinran further clarifies the meaning of visualization of the Buddha, in his *Hymns of the Pure Land*, in this way:

> When sentient beings think on Amida
> Just as a child thinks of its mother,
> They indeed see the Tathagata—who is never distant
> —Both in the present and in the future.[3]

This hymn is based on a passage from the *Sutra of the Samādhi of Heroic Advance*, in which visualization of the Buddha is described in this way:

> If sentient beings are mindful of Amida Buddha and

> say the Name, without fail they will see the Buddha in the present and in the future.[4]

Shinran comments on this sutra passage by saying,

> If sentient beings are mindful of Amida Buddha and say the Name ... [b]oth in this life and in the future they will see the Buddha without fail.[5]

In Shinran's thought, *shinjin* is the experience of awakening, which means that one encounters the Buddha and hears the Buddha's calling voice.

Shinjin as Knowing

There is a third difference between belief, faith, and the Buddhist notion of *shin*. We may believe in something even when we do not understand it fully. However, we cannot believe in something that we are utterly incapable of understanding. Our belief in something must be based on some kind of proof. Faith, on the other hand, surpasses all rationality or intellectual judgment. As I mentioned earlier, however, in Buddhism, *shinjin* or *prasāda* is the experience of awakening, which coincides with *samādhi*. In a certain sense, then, it comes about as our mental function deepens. It does not require that we believe in something as we surrender our intellect or that we have faith in something precisely because it is irrational. This is the fundamental nature of *shin* in Buddhism, especially so in the case when we entrust ourselves to Amida Buddha.

The late Nakamura Hajime, a professor at the University of Tokyo, authored many texts, including one entitled *Ways of Thinking by Eastern Peoples*.[6] According to him, the Indian religions, which include Buddhism, Jainism, and Brahmanism, are all strongly intellectual or philosophical in nature. *Shin*, as expounded in Eastern thought, should be understood as an intellectual term meaning "knowing." In the final analysis, the underlying meaning of *shin* in the Buddhist teaching is "to see the truth." *Shinjin* is identical with true insight, or literally, "knowing and seeing."

Shinjin in Shin Buddhism

Shinjin in Shinran's Thought

Shinjin That Is Wisdom

We will now take a look at Shinran's perspective on *shinjin*. I previously mentioned that *prasāda* was the original word for *shinjin*, or entrusting in Amida Buddha, in the *Larger Sutra of Immeasurable Life*. This refers to a heart and mind that is pure, serene, and peaceful, giving rise to joy. Such *shinjin* is non-dualistic and subjective in nature. It is an experience of awakening, which coincides with *samādhi*. For that reason, *shinjin* is not inconsistent with understanding. Rather, *shinjin* represents the deepening of our mental functioning.

Let me discuss this a little further. Shinran describes *shinjin* with expressions such as "the wisdom of *shinjin*,"[7] "*shinjin* that is wisdom,"[8] or, "the emergence of the mind of entrusting oneself to [Amida's Vow] is the arising of *shinjin*."[9] Wisdom (which I spoke of earlier as *prajñā*) is connected to awakening or the realm of ultimate enlightenment, which Gautama Buddha realized and which is the aim of the Buddhist path. It further coincides in meaning with *samādhi*. Hence, in Shinran's thought, *shinjin* means that we understand in a way that is totally subjective. Of course, understanding here is not a mere intellectual understanding or discrimination. Rather, it is an understanding, or comprehension, that takes place at the deepest "spiritual" dimensions of our religious life.

Shinjin as Awakening

Since our discussion is liable to become a little theoretical, I would like to start it out by reflecting on an experience that I had a long time ago. It happened in a rural farming village in Japan where my temple is located.

At that time, a young woman, who lived in the vicinity of my temple, shared this story with me. She was the mother of a young and very unruly boy. Her son would always boss around the neighborhood children. He would make fun of the other children and would constantly bully them. As a result, the young mother always had to go around to the people in her neighborhood to apologize for her son's behavior. She racked her brains over what to do about her son's unruliness.

One day, when her son was playing with other children, he took a large stick and struck a small child on the head, causing the child to bleed profusely. This caused a huge uproar in the neighborhood. The mother finally could not take it anymore and she lost her temper. She began scolding her son, yelling at him in a loud voice. With that, the boy became very frightened and started to cry. This, however, did not calm the young mother down. She grabbed her son and took him over to the well next to their house. (Long ago in rural farming villages, everyone would dig a well near their house so that they could draw up their own water.) The young mother grabbed hold of her crying son and brought him to their well. There, she held him out right over the mouth of the well and shook him, saying, "I don't want a son like you! You always do nothing but bad things. So, I am going to throw you into this well! But, if you will finally listen to me and tell me that you will never do anything bad again, then I will forgive you. What are you going to do?" The unruly boy had never been scolded in such a terrifying way before. It surprised him and so he stopped crying.

The boy, who was still being held by his mother directly over the well, stared intently into her face. This made the mother think, "Good! This scolding has really worked well." So, once again she said, "Are you going to stop doing bad things? If you keep doing bad things, I am going to throw you into the well!" But at that, the boy, still being held in his mother's arms, said this: "All right, Mom. If you are going to throw me in, then see if you can throw me in!"

As she was telling me this story, the young mother wept and complained, "That's how bad my child is! I just can't control him!" However, as I listened to her story, this is what I was thinking: "Ah! You are describing the bonds between a parent and child. This is what it means to be bound by love!" The boy completely understood the love that his mother had for him. This was something that he understood with his body, in his everyday experience with her and at that moment as well. No matter how severely the young mother might scold her son, her hands could never let go of her child. The child knew this—he understood it perfectly—with his body and throughout his entire being. Hence, he was able to say what he did. In a worldly sense, we might talk about the depth of the trust shared by a parent and child, saying that a child believes in the parent and the parent believes in the child. However, this incident did not take place merely at the level of feelings or emotion.

At a much, much deeper level of knowing, the boy understood his mother's love experientially, literally with his body. This story shows that this kind of understanding can take place in interpersonal relationships in the secular world.

In Shinran's thought, *shinjin* means to understand. Although the story I have related does not point to exactly the same thing, I believe it helps us to see that *shinjin* means that we become able to know. We come to understand at the most profound depths of our consciousness, in a way that is completely subjective and experiential, based on the continuous practice of the *nembutsu* in everyday life. That is also the meaning of *prasāda*. I believe that this is also what Shinran meant when he said,

> Should I have been deceived by Master Hōnen and, saying the nembutsu, were to fall into hell, even then I would have no regrets.[10]

Shinran understood perfectly that he would attain birth in the Pure Land through the *nembutsu*. While such understanding still surpasses our normal sense of logic, it is not illogical in the sense that one risks all in hopeful reliance that birth will take place.

The Japanese language clearly distinguishes between

knowing or understanding with one's mind (intellectually) and knowing or understanding with one's body (experientially). That is to say, knowing in a simple, abstract way is different from knowing through experience. In order to express the notion of knowing or understanding with the body, that is, experiential knowing, the Japanese often say things such as "we experience a deep recollection and realize the truth of something long forgotten" (*omoiataru*) or "we understand something so deeply that we are convinced of its reality beyond any doubt" (*fu ni ochiru*).

The latter expression (*fu ni ochiru*) draws upon the idea of human internal organs, specifically the viscera or guts (*fu*). It means that one understands or is able to comprehend at the bottom of one's guts. The former expression (*omoiataru*) means that one understands or is convinced of some matter through one's experience.

For instance, there is an ancient Japanese saying that goes, "Our parents' benevolence is higher than a mountain and deeper than the sea." Any person from Japan is familiar with this saying. Yet, most people probably only understand it with their minds, as some kind of intellectual knowledge. However, if we live our lives seriously there will doubtlessly be a moment when we come to reflect upon and deeply experience, or become fully convinced of, the meaning of those words. "Ah! That was it! That's what the saying,

'Our parents' benevolence is higher than a mountain and deeper than the sea meant!" It is then that we will understand those words experientially, in a way that penetrates to the very depths of our guts. This is not simply understanding with our minds. Rather, in this way we know or understand—bodily, experientially, and subjectively— through our entire being. This is expressed in the Japanese language as *omoiataru* or *fu ni ochiru*. It is also the meaning of *prasāda* or *shinjin*.

We can come to understand in this way at the most fundamental place in our hearts and minds—at the locus of our personal subjectivity—through the continuous practice of the *nembutsu* in everyday life. Earlier, I talked about this *nembutsu* as living each and every day. This is the sense in which we can say that, in Shinran's thought, *shinjin* means that we awaken. *Shinjin* is the experience of awakening.

Shinjin as Becoming

As I have just mentioned, Shinran's idea of *shinjin* inherited the fundamental Buddhist notion of *shin*. Thus, for instance, even when we say, "I entrust in Amida Buddha," it does not mean that I (as subject) entrust in Amida Buddha (as object) in a dualistic or objectifying way. Rather, I (as subject) become Amida Buddha (as object), and at the same time, Amida Buddha (as object)

Shinjin

becomes me (as subject). That is to say, *shinjin* is the experience of awakening, in which I actually realize that there is no Amida Buddha apart from me; I realize that I am constantly living the life of Amida Buddha, together with Amida Buddha.

Shinran gives an extremely detailed explanation of true and real *shinjin* in "The Chapter on *Shinjin*" of his major work *The True Teaching, Practice, and Realization of the Pure Land Way*. Even there, however, he never says that it occurs in relationship to some object. The only issue that he discusses is the state and nature of one's heart and mind. In contrast, Shinran's other writings and letters are written in a manner intended to be easier for all people to understand. In those works, it follows, he often talks about entrusting in something. Even in those latter works, however, it is important to note that he never uses such objective expressions when he explains *shinjin* in a precise, logical, or doctrinal manner. There he solely, and clearly, explains that one's own heart and mind—one's own personal subjectivity—is transformed anew in the experience of awakening.

In Shinran's thought, *shinjin* means that our own hearts and minds—our own personal subjectivity and our own lives—cast off their old skin and grow anew. As our old skin is cast off, we become new selves. This is what I meant when I said that *shinjin* could also be referred to as awakening. To that I might add that *shinjin* in Shinran's thought also means that we become our true selves.

Traditional Approaches to *Shinjin*

Past Interpretations of *Shinjin*

This way of understanding *shinjin* differs from traditional interpretations of Shin Buddhism. After the death of Shinran, there followed a long period of Shin Buddhist scholasticism in which the study of Shin doctrine was pursued in a variety of ways. In the history of Shin Buddhist doctrinal studies, which is close to eight hundred years in length, interpretations as to *shinjin* could largely be divided into two schools of thought.

The first school of thought takes the position that *shinjin* is a totally non-dualistic and subjective experience of awakening. As I stated above, this represents the fundamental Buddhist understanding of *shinjin*. Thus, if one's approach to Shinran's thought is based on an accurate understanding of Buddhist doctrine, one will naturally and inevitably arrive at this position. The basic stance taken here is that, even while Amida Buddha exists far away from us, Amida does not exist apart from us. *Shinjin* is recognized to be a profound awakening to the existence of Amida Buddha, an existence that is identical with our own.

The other school of thought, in contrast, is not based upon this understanding of Buddhist doctrine. Instead, it was originally intended to make the religious institution of Shin Buddhism abide by the order of Japanese society of that day. Hence, it sought to bring *shinjin* to the level of a secular form of belief. In order to read the passages of Shinran's works in that way, this school interprets *shinjin* to be a dualistic and objectifying kind of belief. That is, Amida Buddha is understood dualistically and objectively to be a Buddha that exists far away from this world, in the distant Pure Land. Despite the complete absence of proof for this assertion, it is held to be unmistakably true, since that is what the sutras and Shinran expound. Or so it is claimed. In other words, this understanding of *shinjin* requires that we simply surrender our intellect and believe without question in a theoretical existence. *Shinjin*, according to this school of thought, is therefore dualistic and objectifying. As such, this understanding of *shinjin* is identical to a general religious notion of faith.

Objective Interpretations of *Shinjin*

This objective interpretation of *shinjin* originated after Shinran's death with the assertions of his great-grandson, Kakunyo (1270-1351), who was the third head priest of the Hongwanji. Kakunyo's approach to *shinjin* was likely influenced by other schools of Pure Land Buddhism, which he had studied in his youth. More important, however, were Kakunyo's designs for the establishment and development of the Hongwanji as a religious organization. This he sought to accomplish by adapting *shinjin* in Shin Buddhism to the societal demands of the rising feudal system of that time.

Shinjin, if grasped dualistically and objectively, could be made to coincide neatly with feudalistic society and its hierarchical social order. Hence, this kind of interpretation of *shinjin* would be favored by anyone seeking to attach importance to worldly affairs and live in obedience to them. For this reason, in the mainstream view of doctrinal studies following Shinran's death, *shinjin* was taken to be a dualistic and objective form of belief. For instance, *shinjin* was considered to be a condition for birth in the Pure Land following one's death. The significance of *shinjin* in present human life was largely overlooked.

It goes without saying that *shinjin* was never considered to be an experience of awakening, or a way of life in which one's old self is cast off and one realizes the growth of a new self. Instead, *shinjin* became a form of intoxication, for it encouraged people to close their eyes to the real contradictions present in their lives and submissively obey the prevailing political system. This can be clearly seen in the understanding of *shinjin* held by Rennyo (1415-1499), the eighth head priest of the Hongwanji. His approach was exclusively dualistic and objectifying, as we can see clearly in his expression "I rely on Amida to save me" (*tasuketamae to tanomu*) and in similar instructions given to his followers. This view completely loses sight of the fact that the Primal Vow of the *Larger Sutra of Immeasurable Life* reveals *shinjin* to be *prasāda*, which is non-dualistic and subjective in nature.

Subjective Understandings of *Shinjin*

Next, let us take a look at some subjective understandings of *shinjin* in Shinran's thought. As we do, we will revisit some of the reasons why *shinjin* in Shin Buddhism, which was originally non-dualistic and subjective, has gradually come to be interpreted as something dualistic and objectifying.

When it is grasped in an entirely subjective way, *shinjin* clearly takes on the meaning of a transcendent, religious experience of awakening. Such an experience inevitably gives rise to a change in the person of *shinjin*. Here, the way in which we live our own lives will naturally, and unavoidably, be brought into question. Living in *shinjin* probes the humanness of our own lives. That is to say, learning within the *nembutsu* and living in *shinjin* means that we (as subjects) become nurtured, little by little, and we are changed, bit by bit, as we become more and more human. As we realize *shinjin*, we awaken. As we awaken, we are nurtured and become our true selves. This is the fundamental meaning of awakening in Buddhism. Buddhist realization signifies that we are able to cast off our old skin and become anew. It means that we are able to become true human beings, little by little. This is not something that happens only after death.

Let me give you an example of what I mean by this. To some people, I am a Buddhist priest. To my child, I am a father. To my neighbors, I am a friend. It truly shames me to admit, however, that I have never been a very good priest, father, or friend. And yet, as I say the *nembutsu* and live in *shinjin* in the midst of these human relationships, this inferior and imperfect self is somehow being nurtured to become a better priest, father, and friend. This is what it means to live while saying the *nembutsu*. This is also what it means when we say that *shinjin* is the non-dualistic and subjective experience of awakening. Shinran points to this sense of becoming when he declares that there are clearly signs (*shirushi*) that one is living in the *nembutsu*.

Also, this kind of subjective understanding of *shinjin* enables us to recognize, in turn, that *shinjin* can be a motivating principle for social action. Inevitably, the way we behave in society will arise from this kind of subjective *shinjin*.

Shinjin

Here is an example. In the late Tokugawa period, the subjective understanding of *shinjin* flourished especially among Shin Buddhist followers in the province of Hiroshima. As direct result of that, very few abortions were carried out in Hiroshima during that time. That is because people understood fully the profound evil involved in the act of taking a young life. During that period many people in farming communities were destitute, and abortions were not uncommon in most of the regions of Japan. However, very few abortions were performed in Hiroshima. Therefore, that province long suffered from overpopulation, and people always had to travel to other areas to find work.

This is the reason why the families of a great many Japanese-Americans originated in Hiroshima. Ever since the United States began to accept Japanese immigrants, people from Hiroshima prefecture have been prominent among those going to America for work. I am also from Hiroshima prefecture, and many persons from my country village, including some of my relatives, emigrated from early on to America, Hawaii, Brazil, and other places. This is an example of the way in which *shinjin* can become a principle that motivates societal behavior among Shin Buddhists. This clearly arose because of the non-dualistic and subjective understanding of *shinjin* in Shin Buddhism.

However, many Shin Buddhist priests find it quite

difficult to preach about this kind of subjective *shinjin*. For many it is too much of a challenge to say that *shinjin* gives rise to self-reformation, that it can become a principle for social action, or that it can lead to the constructing of a new society. What if a priest were to say that, by living within the *nembutsu* and in *shinjin*, we could turn away from our old existence and toward a new humanness, by casting off our old skin and realizing true growth? The priest would probably soon grow wearied of being asked, "What about you? Has it already happened to you?" It is for that reason that Shin Buddhist priests instead preach to us that we will become Buddhas after we die. It is much easier for them to say that. Of course, no one knows what happens after we die. So, priests can say anything they want to about it.

As a result, both the current Shin Buddhist religious organizations and their priests keep a respectful distance away from any subjective understandings of *shinjin*. Any understanding of *shinjin* that is simply dualistic and objective, on the other hand, is welcomed. Throughout all periods of history, there have been people who obediently submitted themselves to the powers that be and their political systems. The only concern for many people was to try to maintain their religious institutions and temples by making them comply with various political and social orders. For them, any non-dualistic or subjective understanding of *shinjin*, which would serve as the principle for social action, posed a dangerous obstacle to their plans.

Therefore, subjective understandings of *shinjin* were always rejected as heresy. Some time ago there were many Shin Buddhist scholars in the Hiroshima region who understood *shinjin* subjectively. However, all of them were labeled as heretics and were punished by the authorities within the Hongwanji organization. My great-grandfather, who was also a Shin Buddhist scholar from that school of thought, was among them. Thus, I think that you can understand some of the reasons why the dualistic and objective understandings of *shinjin* still prevail within the traditional doctrinal studies of the Hongwanji organization today.

However, as we have already seen above, *shinjin* in Shinran's thought, which coincides with the Buddhist notion of shin, is clearly non-dualistic and subjective. That is the fundamental nature of *shinjin*. I believe that we must learn of *shinjin* by returning to the underlying meaning of the Buddhist teachings, to the fundamental purport of the *Larger Sutra of Immeasurable Life*, and to Shinran's basic intent.

Nishida Kitaro (1870-1945), a well-known Japanese philosopher, touched upon Shinran's view of *shinjin* in the very last essey that he wrote.

> If it were to mean that one sees the Buddha

objectively, then the teaching of the Buddha would be the teaching of the devil.[11]

Those of us who are learning about Shin Buddhism should take note of and listen closely to these words.

The Threefold *Shinjin* of the Primal Vow

Three Minds of the Primal Vow

Amida Buddha unceasingly takes in and holds all beings, so as to nurture them to attain enlightenment. This fundamental wish or aspiration of Amida Buddha is called "the Primal Vow." Although we have already taken a look at the content of that Primal Vow, let me rephrase it here.

> All beings! If you hear Amida Buddha's Name—that calling voice—with a true mind (sincere mind), entrusting (mind of entrusting), and wishing to be born in the Pure Land (desire for birth), and throughout your lives saying the nembutsu, then, no matter how serious the karmic evil that you commit may be, I will enable all of you to realize birth in the Pure Land and attain Buddhahood. If this should not be fulfilled, I will not realize the enlightenment of the Buddha.[12]

Shinjin

In order to be born in the Pure Land and attain enlightenment, it is essential that we call the Buddha's Name (Amida Buddha's naming of itself), and with a threefold mind of sincerity, entrusting, and desire for birth, live our lives by saying the *nembutsu* each and every day. This represents Amida Buddha's aspiration for us. Shinran later explained that "sincere mind, entrusting, and desire for birth," while all different, are fundamentally identical in meaning. They all refer to true and real *shinjin*. That is, the three minds of the Primal Vow—sincere mind, entrusting mind, and the mind desiring birth—all constitute *shinjin*.

Three Aspects of *Shinjin*

Let us now take a look at Shinran's interpretation of these three aspects of *shinjin*.

Shinran speaks of the "threefold *shinjin* of the Primal Vow" in his text *Notes on 'Essentials of Faith Alone.'*[13] That is, he says that there are three aspects to *shinjin*. He then offers an identical analysis for each of the three minds (sincere mind, entrusting, and desire for birth) of the Primal Vow. In that way, he implies that each of them actually constitutes *shinjin*. It is not that there are three kinds of *shinjin*. Rather, Shinran reveals the nature of a single *shinjin* by grasping it from three perspectives.

Further, Shinran cites a variety of terms when he

addresses the meaning of *shinjin* in his texts. Among all of them, the terms "deep mind," "true mind," and "mind of aspiration" are noteworthy since they each provide a clear and straightforward description of the distinctive nature of *shinjin* in the Shin Buddhist teaching. I believe that these three terms also correspond to the threefold mind of the Primal Vow in this way:

>True mind—sincere mind
>Deep mind—entrusting
>Mind of aspiration—desire for birth.

In the next chapter, we will look concretely at the content of *shinjin,* based on a discussion of these three minds.

Chapter Three

Deep Mind, True Mind, and Mind of Aspiration

Deep Mind

Psychological Perspective

We will now look at the first aspect of *shinjin*: deep mind (*jinshin*). This term appears as one of the three minds expounded in the *Sutra on the Contemplation of [the Buddha of] Immeasurable Life*. As we have seen earlier, it also corresponds to the mind of entrusting in the passage of the Primal Vow. In Shinran's understanding, this deep mind has the meaning of "true and real *shinjin*."

Deep mind represents true and real *shinjin* when seen

from a psychological perspective. As I have been saying repeatedly, *shinjin* is the experience of awakening. Awakening has a cognitive sense, which from a psychological point of view constitutes an extraordinarily deep mind. A person with a shallow mind approaches life in a superficial or frivolous way. Such a person is only able to see the exterior of an object and is thus unable to gain a clear perception of its true nature. In contrast, the person who lives with a deep mind is constantly delving deeply into his own mind and is able to discover much there. For Shinran, entrusting in the Buddha means that one lives with this kind of deep mind. Thus, in Shin Buddhism *shinjin* is the experience of deep and profound awakening.

One *nembutsu* follower who deeply lived within this *shinjin* was Asahara Saichi (1850-1932) of Shimane prefecture in Japan. Here is one of his poems.

> Saichi is a pitiful fellow.
> Standing before the Tathagata,
> I smelled something horrible,
> And when I looked closely,
> I saw that the Buddha was on fire!
> So I beat out the flames.
> It was a dream I had last night,
> And so after I awoke, I bowed in worship.
> Oh, I have false views about everything.

Shinjin

> How pitiful! How pitiful!
> Namuamidabutsu. Namuamidabutsu.

This is the story about a dream that Saichi had one night. In his dream, he was standing before the Buddhist altar (*butsudan*) when he smelled something burning. He looked carefully around the butsudan and came upon the painted image of the Buddha. He was shocked to see that the Buddha's feet were burning. So, he quickly patted out the fire on the painting. Soon after, he suddenly awoke from the dream and got out of his bed. He immediately went to the *butsudan*, opened its doors, and began to worship before it fervently. Saichi realized that his heart and mind was filled with false views as to all matters; thus he was constantly burning up the Buddha's heart. Awakening in shame to his pitiful self, he could only recite, "Namuamidabutsu. Namuamidabutsu."

Here, in Saichi's fervent utterance of the *nembutsu*, we hear the moaning voice of one who is peering directly into the world of hell, which lies concealed within the depths of his own heart. These words allow us to reflect on the boundless depths of the heart and mind of Saichi, this "wondrous, excellent person" of *shinjin* (*myōkōnin*).

Shan-tao (613-681), a leading figure in Chinese Pure Land Buddhism, wrote that "deep mind is the deeply entrusting mind."[14] He then went on to explain that there are two aspects to this deeply entrusting mind. The first means that we reflect upon our actual state, and know deeply that we are beings whose karmic evil is immense and heavy. Hence, we will never be able to escape from this world, which is not-real, empty, and false. The second aspect is that, through learning the Buddha-dharma, we deeply know that Amida Buddha exists especially for such beings as ourselves, and that when we say the *nembutsu* we are always embraced by that Buddha's great compassion throughout our lives.

In this way, deep mind signifies that we profoundly know our selves and the Buddha. These two kinds of knowing do not arise independently of each other. Instead, they always exist in simultaneous identity with each other. It is when our ego-selves are continuously brought sharply and deeply into question and are thereby cast aside, that the Buddha becomes manifest within our selves. And, at the same time that the Buddha becomes manifest, our ego-selves are all the more deeply brought into question and are discarded.

Here is an example. Imagine that we are digging into the ground in search of water. We find that as we dig deeper and deeper into the earth, more and more pure water springs forth from its depths. The deeper we dig, the more water streams forth. At the same time, however, we also find that, as more and more water streams out from the

Shinjin

earth, it is causing our hole in the ground to grow deeper and deeper. The flowing water itself is digging deeply into the ground from below. In the same way, the more we look within and question our own existence, the more the Buddha becomes manifest before us—coming to us, as it were, from the opposite direction. These two kinds of knowing, which come from completely opposite directions, intersect within us.

We can explain this further through the example of shadow and light. The darkness of my own shadow becomes visible when my figure is exposed by the warm, brilliant light. Both light and shadow exist at the same time. Because the light reaches me, the image of my shadow appears. My shadow appears because I am now illuminated by the light. Although light and shadow exist in contrast to each other, they really exist in simultaneous identity.

The darkness of my shadow becomes visible for the first time when I am exposed to the light. My shadow cannot occur by itself, in the absence of light. It is because I am immersed in the light that my shadow will unfailingly be produced. I have a shadow because at this very moment I am the recipient of light. Light and shadow, which are totally contrary to each other, come about at the same time. This is the structure of the deep mind.

In Shinran's writings, a variety of terms are used to describe this. D. T. Suzuki calls it the "logic of *prajñā*." This "logic of *prajñā*" is the fundamental logic of Mahayana Buddhism. Shinran expresses it as "attaining enlightenment without severing blind passions" (*bonnō soku bodai*) and "samsara is the same as nirvana" (*shōji soku nehan*). Suzuki also describes this logic with the phrase "A equals not A." A is identical with that which is not A. That is, two things that are the complete opposites of each other—two things that mutually contradict each other (A and not-A)—occur at the same time as identical things. This is the logic of wisdom or enlightenment, as it is set forth in Mahayana Buddhism. However, this logic is not just simple wordplay or abstract speculation. If that were so, then it would be completely meaningless. Rather, this logic becomes true and real for the first time when we experience it with our entire existence and when it forms the inner reality of that experience of awakening, or, deep mind.

I am sure that we are all very grateful for the kind benevolence that our parents have bestowed on us. We know that our parents underwent great hardship and made many sacrifices on our behalf. Yet, we are able to awaken deeply to the benevolence of our parents only when we see the dark shadows of our many unfilial acts and we are filled with shame. Neither aspect can occur by itself. Thoughts of gratitude for our parents' benevolence become identical with tears of remorse, which flow as we reflect deeply on the considerable trouble that we caused them and the many times that we were unfilial. This is the way in which we come to understand our parents' love for us. These two kinds of realization are absolutely contrary to each other. And yet, they take place at the same time within us. Awakening is that kind of experience.

Allow me to give you another example. We have all probably had the experience of waking up in the middle of a dream and realizing, "Ah! That was a dream!" This, of course, is what we commonly call the experience of waking up. However, even this experience implies that two completely opposite events—dreaming and waking—have occurred at virtually the same time. Shinran explains that the structure of *shinjin*, or deep mind, is based on the same logic. The Buddha's great compassion does not exist apart from our realization of our own defiled passions and karmic sins. Great compassion exists, necessarily, when it takes in our karmic sins.

The most detailed descriptions of hell in Pure Land Buddhism are found in the *Essentials for Attaining Birth* by Genshin (942–1017). There he states that the most frightening of all the hells into which we must fall is Avici Hell, which lies in the ultimate depths of the earth. He describes it as the black, dark world, which we finally reach after falling headfirst toward the bottom of the earth for two thousand years. This realm of hell represents the dark, black nature of our own hearts and minds. We can come to know it for the first time only when we bore deeply into our selves and look directly into the very depths of our own hearts and minds.

When I read this passage in my younger days, I was moved by Genshin's profound understanding of hell. Because of what I have been taught by Genshin, I do not ask whether the realm of hell exists or not. To me, the question that needs to be asked is whether we are able to see it or not.

One Who Is Falling into Hell

Some time ago I had the following experience. I had been invited to give a Dharma talk at a Buddhist temple in Japan. When the talk was finished and I was resting, a gentleman came over and indicated that he wanted to speak with me. I did not know the gentleman, but when I asked him what he wanted, this is what he said.

"My father died when I was very young, and my mother had to work very hard to raise me all by herself. My mother was a woman who lived in very deep *shinjin*. She was always going around to temples in order to listen to the Buddha-dharma. She also worshipped every day before our family's *obutsudan* and spent her days living in the *nembutsu*. My mother, however, was in the habit of saying the same thing over and over again, 'I am falling headfirst

Shinjin

into hell, you know. How shameful it is! How shameful!'

"I never could understand how she could listen to the teachings of the Buddha so often and say the *nembutsu* all the time, and yet still say that she was going to hell. I thought that she should not say such strange things, for I believed that someone like my mother would surely be able to avoid falling into hell and would gain birth in the Pure Land. Perhaps it was too close to me then. Also, at that time I had no interest in the Buddha-dharma. So I never asked my mother why she said what she did.

"After my mother passed away and I grew older, I started to go to the temple to listen to the Buddha-dharma, just like my mother had, for my mind was troubled by the words that she had constantly uttered, 'I am going to hell, you know.' I always worried about where my mother was—whether she had indeed fallen into hell. It always weighed heavily on my mind. However, after hearing your talk today, Sensei, I am finally able to understand. I am truly happy to know without any doubt that my mother is in the Pure Land. So, I came here because I wanted to express my thanks to you."

According to my understanding of the *nembutsu* and *shinjin*, we will never realize birth in the Pure Land unless we pass through hell. It is not as if the Pure Land is over to the right and hell is over to the left. Rather, I believe that we are able to be born in the Pure Land only when we awaken to the depth of our own defiled passions, the weight of our own karmic evil, and the fact that there is nothing we can do but fall into hell. Shinran stared intently and deeply into himself and said, "I will surely fall into hell." And yet, at the same time, he was also able to say, "My birth in the Pure Land is assured." He was sure—for him, it was settled —that he would fall into hell and be born in the Pure Land. Logically, this is a contradiction, for it means that two complete opposites are settled at the same time. Yet, this is the inner reality of *shinjin* or deep mind. This is the logic of A=not-A. It is also represented by the relationship between light and shadow. This is how I comprehend *shinjin* in Shin Buddhism: only the person who deeply awakens to the truth that "I can only go to hell" will truly be able to attain birth in the Pure Land.

These are the thoughts that I shared with that gentleman. As I listened to his story, I felt quite happy and grateful in knowing that there was a person whose thoughts and understanding were similar to my own. And, from him, I was able to learn once again about the deep mind of *shinjin*.

What Is *Tariki*?

As we have seen, in Shin Buddhism, one aspect of *shinjin* is deep mind. Let us now consider the connection between this deep mind and *tariki* (which is usually translated into English literally as "Other Power").

Previously, I said that deep mind represents the world that we come to see for the first time when we delve deeply into our own hearts and minds. It is just as if we were to dig a hole in the ground in search of water. The deeper we bore into the earth, the more pure water will spring forth from the opposite direction. And, the greater the force with which that water gushes up, the deeper the hole in the earth will grow. Or, when we strike a ball toward the ground, the harder that we hit the ball, the higher the ball will fly up from the ground into the air.

In the same way, the deeper we delve into our hearts and minds, while saying the *nembutsu*, the more we will be able to perceive our defiled passions and our shadowy hearts of self-attachment. And at exactly the same time, the life and heart of the Buddha come to make themselves known to us. Here, two opposing realities reveal themselves at the same time, from completely opposite directions. Earlier I spoke of the logic of A=not-A. *Shinjin* is the experience in which two things, which are in absolute contradictory opposition to each other, arise in simultaneous identity. In Shin Buddhism, we use the idea of *tariki* simply in order to explain this basic reality of *shinjin*. It means nothing more than that.

Earlier, we saw that the idea of "entrusting in the

Buddha" does not imply that the Buddha first exists as a precondition to all things, and we thereupon believe in that existence. Rather, it means that we live our lives, earnestly saying the *nembutsu* and realizing *shinjin* in accord with that *nembutsu*, and the Buddha's existence is manifested with complete certainty for us within our *shinjin*. In Shin Buddhism, this is the structure of *shinjin*.

I also mentioned that the only path leading to birth in the Pure Land is the one that leads us in the direction of hell. A related expression can be seen in the *Mahā Parinirvāṇa Sutra*, which teaches of "*shinjin* that has no root in my heart." True *shinjin* is without roots. Yet, even without roots, its stem still grows, its leaves lengthen, and its flowers bloom. The flower of *shinjin* blooms beautifully, even though it has no roots in our hearts. Shinran cites the passage from the *Maha Parinirvaṇa Sutra* that contains this expression for *shinjin*. A similar phrase, which can be found in *A Record in Lament of Divergences* (*Tannishō*), is "*shinjin* given by Amida."[15] These two expressions mean the same thing.

The Buddha's heart and life are nowhere to be found within our own. Instead, our own lives and hearts contain nothing but defiled passions and the conditions to fall into hell. In them, there is not even the tiniest speck of the true Pure Land. Our lives always run counter to Amida Buddha. And yet, despite that, in the *nembutsu* and *shinjin* the

Buddha's life becomes manifested—inconceivably—within our own lives. The wondrous light of the Pure Land bursts into our own hearts and minds. This coincides with the logic of A=not-A, which I will rephrase as, "It is not and thus it is." In other words, something that ought not to exist exists inconceivably, in the truest sense. *The Mahā Parinirvāṇa Sutra* describes this as "*shinjin* that has no root in my heart" and the Tannishō offers the phrase "*shinjin* given by Amida."

"It is not and thus it is." That which is not within me exists within me. The only way for us to express this paradoxical logic is to say that something is "given by" or "received from" another. Thus, we use the expression "*tariki*." This does not in any way mean that some power from an other moves toward us in a physical sense. Rather, *tariki* allows us to express the logic that is latent within the very profound experience of *shinjin*.

Even though it speaks in terms of "power," *tariki* explicates the logical structure of *shinjin*, which, as we have seen earlier, is one of "It is not and thus it is." For those who have not experienced *shinjin*, this would seem to be nothing more than an utterly abstract expression or concept. Any discussion of *tariki* removed from the experience of *shinjin* would be totally meaningless. This point needs to be made clear at the outset. Now, we can take a closer look at the idea of *tariki*.

Conditional Arising and *Tariki*

T'an-luan (476-542) of China was the first person to use the word *tariki* in the history of Pure Land Buddhism. The original Sanskrit term may have been present in the various sutras and commentaries that were translated by Bodhiruci (ca. fifth to sixth centuries C.E.) of India. T'an-luan learned the Pure Land teachings from those Chinese translations. It is often asked what the Sanskrit origin of the word *tariki* might have been. At the present time, the answer is not clear. It has long been said that it might have been the word *paratantra*, and it is so noted in Nakamura Hajime's *Bukkyōgo Daijiten* (Dictionary of Buddhist Terms). This, however, is looked upon with some doubt by today's scholars. Hence, as of now, the origin of the word *tariki* is not clear.

My personal view, however, is that *tariki* was probably based on the concept of *paratantra*, as it has been long claimed, or upon some other closely related term. The word paratantra was translated into Chinese as *engi* (conditional arising) or *eta* (depending on others). I believe that, although its origin might have been somewhat different, the notion of *tariki* also developed out of the concept of *engi*. Conditional arising (sometimes called "dependent origination") is a fundamental tenet of Buddhism. *En* can also be found in the term *in-en* (causes and conditions).

Here, *in* refers to a cause.

In order for a cause to bring about an effect, it is also necessary that there be a wide variety of indirect activities. Such indirect activity is referred to as *en*, or conditions. When the causes and conditions are in harmony the result can come about. In this sense, this world and all things in it come to exist through the interrelationship, or combination, of infinite causes and conditions. Although the direct cause is important, the indirect conditions are even more important. A single cause might result in many differing effects, depending upon the presence and nature of different conditions. Thus, Buddhism teaches that conditions are very significant. All phenomena in this world and human life come about as the result of causes and conditions. This is called *engi* (conditional arising).

For example, let us say that I am now presenting a lecture to you and other students. The direct causes that are bringing about this phenomenon are you and me. Each student in our class is a cause. I am also a cause. All of these causes join together to form this class and, as a result, we can all learn together. However, our lecture has not come about simply because of you and me.

Our lecture is also the result of the efforts of those who planned and coordinated it. It is also due to the support of our school and its teaching staff. In addition, you, the other students, and I are able to be present at this lecture because of a wide range of events, people, and things, both visible and invisible. All of these activities that are supporting us at this moment—the indirect causes that have brought about this phenomenon—are what we refer to as conditions. Thus, the phenomenon of this lecture is occurring at this present moment as the result of the combining of all of these countless causes and conditions. This is the meaning of conditional arising. There is absolutely no phenomenon that takes place in isolation. All things arise through a multitude of interrelationships.

Let us describe this a little more concretely. Because you and the other students have attended this lecture today, I am also here. If, for instance, I had come here to teach, but no students were present, today's lecture would not have taken place. Or, conversely, if all of you had assembled here, but I had not come because I was ill, this lecture would not have occurred. This present moment takes place within the relationship between you, the other students, and me. This is also conditional arising.

The notion of *paratantra* means that the existence of one thing depends upon another. In terms of our present discussion, if I were to say, "I am giving a lecture, and so you are here," this I would reflect a very egocentric way of thinking. Any claim that "I stand before you" would be a very non-Buddhist way of thinking. Rather, it is only because of you that I now exist. If you were not here, I would not now exist. This is the way of thinking found in Buddhism, which severely cautions us against pursuing an egocentric or self-centered way of life.

As I gain an even deeper understanding of conditional arising in Buddhism, I come to realize that the phenomenon of this lecture is now taking place for my sake, due solely to you and the other students. In other words, it is occurring as a result of an "other." I believe that here is where the notion of *tariki* arose. Once again, this is only speculation on my part. Still, I believe that the idea of *tariki* came about in relation to a deepening understanding of the concept of conditional arising.

Religion as Path

Previously we discussed the structure of Amida Buddha's Primal Vow. Amida Buddha's becoming Amida Buddha (that is, Amida's attainment of Buddhahood) and our attainment of Buddhahood are identical to each other and occur at the same time. According to the Buddhist principle of conditional arising, that is how it must occur. However, in our current state of being, we are really always moving away from truth and the Buddha. Our lives are pointed in only one direction—the direction of hell.

In theory, the principle of conditional arising provides that our attainment of Buddhahood and the Buddha's attainment of Buddhahood are identical and simultaneous. However, when we face our actual selves and see the way we really are right now, we cannot avoid thinking that the process of conditional arising (and our attainment of Buddhahood) is solely due to an "other"—the working of Amida Buddha. In Shin Buddhism, *shinjin* or deep mind is expressed as "*shinjin* that has no root in my heart" or "*shinjin* that is given to us by the Buddha." I have described the structure of this *shinjin* with the phrase "It is not and thus it is." *Tariki* does nothing more than give expression to this logical structure of *shinjin*. This functioning, however, does not exist for the *shinjin* of *jiriki* (self-power), which stands opposite of *tariki* (Other Power). For in self—power, the egocentric self still survives, unabandoned.

Thus, in Shin Buddhism when we say, "I am saved by Amida Buddha," this essentially means that, at the very moment that Amida Buddha attains Buddhahood, we are saved and attain Buddhahood, through conditional arising. Conversely, when we are saved, Amida Buddha attains Buddhahood. It is not that Amida Buddha first attains enlightenment and becomes a Buddha, and then later the Buddha's Vow and power come to save us. Yet, in spite of this structure of simultaneous identity in the Primal Vow, we still feel that we are constantly going contrary to and running away from Amida Buddha. That is how we experience *shinjin*. For such persons as us, *shinjin* is experienced as a completely unilateral activity of Amida Buddha, which moves toward us.

Again, in Shin Buddhism *tariki* is a description of the logic of the innermost reality of this religious experience of deep *shinjin*. However, in the past and even now there are persons whose understanding of *tariki* is shallow and who consider it to be a form of power. This is a complete misunderstanding.

There are many different religions in the world. If we were to try to classify them, we might first of all say that there are religions that speak of the exclusive power and might of a transcendent being. They teach that such a power can deliver a variety of benefits to us. Many religions in the world correspond to this type of "religion of power."

On the other hand, there are also religions that speak of universal or global principles. They teach that true human life is established when one learns those principles and lives in accordance with them. The Buddhist teaching, as revealed by Gautama Buddha, corresponds to this type of "religion as path." However, as Buddhism was transmitted from India to China and Japan, it encountered various regional religions, most of which were religions of power. As it merged with those religions, Buddhism changed in large measure into a religion of power as well. As he learned the Pure Land teachings and the path of the *nembutsu*, Shinran earnestly wished to return to the original

Buddhist teachings of Gautama Buddha. Hence, he completely did away with those aspects derived from religions of power and clearly established that the Shin Buddhist path to enlightenment is a religion as path.

However, following the death of Shinran, the Shin Buddhist teaching of the *nembutsu* became enmeshed in various ways with Shintō, which is a Japanese religion of power. This is the situation even today. In this regard, it is important that we reflect critically on past history and seek to return truly to the fundamental purport of Shinran. The fact that, even today, some still view *tariki* as some kind of power is a reflection of the "Shintō-ization" of Shin Buddhism. This is another point of which we need to be fully aware, as we study Shin Buddhism. The teaching of Shinran—the Shin Buddhist path to enlightenment—is not in any way a religion of power. It is a religion as path—the path of awakening, in which we earnestly say the *nembutsu* and attain Buddhahood, realizing growth and maturity as true human beings.

True Mind

Philosophical Perspective

Next, I would like to speak to you about the second aspect of *shinjin*: true mind (*shinshin*). The term, true mind, appears to have originated in the writings of Shan-tao of China. It corresponds to sincere mind, which is found within the threefold mind of the Primal Vow in the *Larger Sutra of Immeasurable Life*, as well as to sincere mind, which is one of the three minds expounded in the *Contemplation Sutra*. Shinran frequently speaks of true and real *shinjin* as "true mind" (*makoto no kokoro* in Japanese).

As I mentioned earlier, when I came to America twenty years ago a Shin Buddhist minister told me that both Christianity and Shin Buddhism were using the word "faith" in the same way, as in "I put my faith in God" or "I put my faith in Buddha." This, I was told, was creating much confusion for people. In response, I explained that Shinran refers to *shinjin* as *shinshin*. I asked the ministers whether this word ought to be translated as "true mind" or "true heart." What do you think? For me, true mind points to the value of *shinjin*. Thus, in contrast to deep mind, which describes *shinjin* from a psychological point of view, we can say the expression "true mind" looks at it from a philosophical perspective.

Shinran often writes of "true and real *shinjin*" and "pure *shinjin*." These can be expressed as "true mind" and "pure mind," respectively. Here, by saying that *shinjin* is true mind, he means that this mind is "not-false." That is, it is completely free of emptiness and falsity. When he says that *shinjin* is pure mind, he means that it is "not-inverted."

That is, it is far removed from this secular world, which is filled with inverted thinking and a lack of thoroughness.

Here Shinran's thinking is based on that of T'an-luan. Purity, he says, is not-inverted and refers to one who is truly in accord with the truth of suchness or dharma-nature. To be true or not-false, he explains, means that one takes in and holds all sentient beings. In other words, when he says that *shinjin* is "pure mind," he is talking about its "self-benefiting" nature, since this mind is in accord with fundamental truth that pervades the world and the universe. When he says that *shinjin* is "true mind," he is referring to its sense of "benefiting others," for this mind embraces all living beings—all "others"—and enables them to enter the realm of truth and reality. In other words, *shinjin* is the mind of living in the truth and working to guide others to that truth. However, Shinran also says that the pure mind of self-benefit and true mind of benefiting others pertain only to the mind of Amida Buddha. Such a mind exists nowhere within us. In reality, the state of our own hearts and minds is always the complete opposite of Amida's heart and mind.

Shinjin, as we have already seen, refers to an experience in which we encounter the Buddha and awaken to the deepest reaches of our hearts and minds. Encountering the Buddha, here, means that Amida Buddha's pure and true mind — the mind that is not-false, not-empty, and not-inverted—is integrated for the first time into our own impure and untrue lives and into our own minds, which are false, empty, and inverted. Thus, *shinjin* will naturally involve a sharp, contradictory opposition between truth and non-truth, purity and impurity, non-invertedness and invertedness, and not-false and falsity.

Again, this contradiction is the logical structure of A = not-A. It also thus gives rise to the recurrence of unrelenting lament and shame. Shinran's writings frequently reveal this with words of scathing self-repentance. And yet, inevitably, when *shinjin* continues to operate in this way, we come to realize that the pure and true mind of the Buddha, as well as the life of the Buddha, have become integrated within our own minds and lives, which remain totally impure and not—true. This is then the inner reality of *shinjin*: as our impure and untrue minds and lives are turned about little by little, they are transformed, through the Buddha's mind and life, into minds and lives that are pure and true.

Transformation of Life

Shinran calls this activity of *shinjin*—in which our impure and untrue minds and lives are made pure and true, little by little—"transformation" (*tenjō*, literally, "turning and becoming"). Our hearts and minds are always not-true and full of lies. However, as we hear the Buddha-dharma on the path of the *nembutsu*, realizing *shinjin* and encountering the Buddha, and, as that *nembutsu* and *shinjin* deepen, then our own personal subjectivity and lives gradually turn from falsity and emptiness into truth and reality. As I mentioned earlier, the structure of *shinjin* is such that we awaken to darkness and light—to hell and the Pure Land—at the same time. However, in actuality, when we live in such *shinjin*, darkness and light, or hell and the Pure Land, do not remain in simple contradictory opposition. Rather, *shinjin* functions to turn darkness into light and transform hell into the Pure Land, little by little.

Shinran explains it in this way:

> "To be transformed" means that evil karma, without being nullified or eradicated, is made into the highest good, just as all waters, upon entering the great ocean,[16] immediately become ocean water.

We live our lives with foolish hearts of defiled passions and shadowy minds that always harbor hell-like thoughts. Even when we live in *shinjin*, we still bear those thoughts and defiled passions. And yet, with our evil karma left unextinguished, our minds and lives are slowly, slowly transformed into the mind of the Buddha and the pure life of the Buddha's Pure Land. It is just like, for example, the waters of many rivers that flow into the sea. No matter how pure or defiled the waters may have been, when they enter the currents of the great ocean they all change into the same, clear ocean water. In a similar passage, Shinran also states,

> Obstructions of karmic evil turn into virtues;
> It is like the relation of ice and water:
> The more the ice, the more the water;
> The more the obstructions, the more the virtues.[17]

Here, "obstructions of karmic evil" refer to defiled passions or the karma generated by our evil offenses. They obstruct our attainment of enlightenment. Yet, those very obstructions, just as they are, become the very substance of virtue, which is the life and enlightenment of the Buddha. It is just like the relationship between ice and water, Shinran declares. The more ice that there is, the more water there will be when the ice melts. In the same way, the more defiled passions and obstructions of karmic evil that we possess, the greater will be the life and enlightenment of the Buddha.

Our lives and karmic evil, and the Buddha's life and enlightenment, are like ice and water, respectively. Through the sun's activity, the ice melts and turns into water. In exactly the same way, when the light of Amida Buddha's wisdom illuminates our lives, the ice of our delusions and karmic evil melts and becomes, just as it is, the water of the Buddha's life and enlightenment. Hence, Shinran says, "The more the ice, the more the water." The deeper our karmic evil, the greater the life of the Buddha will be. As I mentioned before, the deeper we dig down into the ground, the more clean water will gush forth from the earth. Or, the harder that one strikes a ball toward the ground, the higher the ball will fly up into the sky in the opposite direction. Relating this to *shinjin* again, the more we realize the depth of our own deluded thinking and karmic evil, the more we will awaken, with gratitude and joy, to the greatness and strength of Amida Buddha's compassionate Vow, which works for each of us.

Our everyday lives are truly humble and mean. Covered with the mud of defiled passions, our lives are of a shadowy darkness. However, when we learn the Buddha—dharma, earnestly say the *nembutsu*, and realize *shinjin*, our lives of darkness change little by little into the pure, luminous life of the Buddha. This is transformation, or turning and becoming. I am not saying that pitch darkness becomes pure brilliance right away. What I am saying is that, just as ice melts bit by bit and becomes water, our lives of defiled passions, emptiness, and falsity are transformed very slowly into the life of the Buddha. We do not discard the ice and fill ourselves up with fresh, new water. Nor do we completely eliminate our evil lives and replace them with

Shinjin

brand new lives. We do not instantly become pure and undefiled. Rather, in the *nembutsu* and *shinjin*, our lives change little by little—we are transformed bit by bit—into the life of the Buddha.

This explanation of transformation is probably difficult to grasp. So, I would like to give you an illustration of what I am trying to say. Are you familiar with dried persimmons? This is a very old haiku poem about dried persimmons.

> Ah! How very sweet!
> Is the bitterness of the
> Bitter persimmon.

Just as in Japan, there are probably places in America where persimmons are gathered in the fall. There are basically two kinds of persimmons: sweet and bitter. Sweet persimmons do not ripen well in cold climates and so most are produced in warmer regions. Bitter persimmons are often so strongly astringent that they are completely inedible. Those that are really bitter are grown in certain colder climates, not in warmer regions. It is said that the sweetest dried persimmons are made from persimmons that are extremely astringent.

There is a top-grade fruit store in the Ginza area of Tokyo that sells dried persimmons for two thousand yen each. These persimmons are rich with natural taste and are truly delicious. Once I asked the shop owner how such delicious dried persimmons are produced. He told me that they are made from the most strongly astringent persimmons gathered in the Northeast region of Japan. After their skins are removed, they are hung out to dry in the cool, late-autumn breeze. There, exposed to the light of the late-autumn sun, the bitterness of the persimmons slowly changes into sweetness. The more bitter they are, the more naturally delicious and sweet they become. This is indeed what the poet meant when he said, "Ah! How very sweet!/Is the bitterness of the/Bitter persimmon." This is also, I believe, the meaning of transformation in Shinran's teaching.

To Die and Be Born

When we live in the *nembutsu* and *shinjin* our lives and our own personal subjectivity are gradually transformed and change bit by bit. Yet, Shinran also talks about *shinjin* in this way:

> Concerning the entrusting of oneself to the Primal Vow, [to borrow the words of Shan-tao,] "in the preceding moment, life ends...." Concerning immediately attaining birth, [to borrow the words of

Shinjin

Shan-tao,] "in the next moment, you are immediately born."[18]

This passage merges the phrase "[Sentient beings] ... realize even one thought—moment of *shinjin* and joy,... they then attain birth," from the passage declaring the fulfillment of the Primal Vow in the *Larger Sutra of Immeasurable Life*,[19] with the passage "... in the preceding moment, life ends... in the next moment, you are immediately born" from Shan-tao's Hymns of Birth in the Pure Land.

In Shan-tao's passage, the word "moment" (*nen*) signifies time. He is discussing one's birth in the Pure Land after death. However, Shinran's passage is meant to describe the realization of *shinjin* in this present life. That is, when we entrust in and awaken to the Primal Vow of Amida Buddha, our lives of delusion come to an end in the moment of time just before *shinjin* arises. In the following moment, we immediately attain birth in this very world. In *shinjin* our lives up until this moment come to an end, and we are born anew into the life of the Buddha. This means that we die to our old selves and are born into new lives.

This, I believe, is a way of explaining the transformation of life within *shinjin* from a different angle. It does not mean, however, that once *shinjin* has arisen it continues straight on throughout life. Although *shinjin* may begin with a "turning of mind" (*eshin*) or the "attaining of *shinjin*" (*gyakushin*), it does not continue on all the way to the end of life. Rather, the experience of awakening (after that initial moment) is realized over and over again, from time to time, as the result of the arising of various conditions within our lives.

Thus, the awakening of *shinjin* is experienced repeatedly and continuously by us in our individual human lives. The passage above speaks to the repetition and continuation of *shinjin* as the experience of awakening. Transformation takes place from time to time so that "in the preceding moment, life ends, and in the next moment, [we] are immediately born." Our old lives come to an end and we are born to new lives. These successive repetitions of transformation take place in what I call "non-continuous continuity." This means that, as we die and are born, and (again) die and are born, we are nurtured and enabled to grow personally as human beings. Hence, *shinjin* in Shinran's thought is both awakening and becoming: we become and realize true growth unceasingly. It shames me to say, however, that although I have been studying the *nembutsu* path of Shin Buddhism for a long time, I have not yet become fully matured or realized true growth as a human being. But, this is the nature of *shinjin* in Shin Buddhism.

Let me share another story with you. Once, there was a

farmer in Shimane prefecture of Japan by the name of Zentaro (1782–1856), who deeply lived a life of *shinjin*. It was said that he had an extremely violent nature. In his younger days, he was a heavy drinker and gambler, and was always getting into brawls. The people of his village hated him and called him "Zentaro the viper." However, he also encountered great tragedy in his life. Each of his children, one after another, died in infancy. As a result of that, he sought after the Buddha-dharma, and finally, it is said, he came to live in very deep *shinjin*.

One summer day, Zentaro went off in the morning into the mountains to cut wood, and in the evening he returned home, carrying the wood on his shoulders. He was covered in sweat, and so, as he always did, Zentaro went to get hot water from the kitchen so that he could clean up. On that day, however, his wife, Toyo, had forgotten to boil the water for his bath, and there was no hot water in the kettle. Having a violent temper, Zentaro shouted out at Toyo with a loud voice and rebuked her. Not liking what Toyo had to say, Zentaro then yelled even louder at her, "You!" He picked up a piece of firewood from the ground and, brandishing it menacingly, started to chase after his wife. He finally trapped Toyo at a corner of the house, where she cowered before him. But, just as Zentaro was about to bring down the stick of wood to strike Toyo, he suddenly let out a loud moan, "Oh!" and abruptly ran into the house. There, he threw himself down in front of the butsudan and placed the stick of wood in front of him, crying out, "Ah! Zentaro's real nature has appeared again!" Then, in a loud voice he recited the *nembutsu*, "Namu Amidabutsu. Namu Amidabutsu."

This story presents us with the image of a Shin Buddhist follower who had been nurtured wonderfully by the *nembutsu*. Here was a person who was undergoing a transformation—a turning and becoming—of dying to his old self and being born anew. In the preceding moment, his old life came to an end, and in the next moment, he was immediately born. As we listen to Zentaro's story we should all deeply and critically reflect upon the way in which we live our own lives every day.

Mind of Aspiration

Ethical Perspective

The third aspect of *shinjin* is the mind of aspiration (*ganshin*). This mind corresponds to the mind that desires birth in the Primal Vow in the *Larger Sutra of Immeasurable Life*. It also may be said to match the mind of aspiration for birth and directing virtue in the *Contemplation Sutra*. Shinran's basic approach was to consider this mind of aspiration to be the mind of Amida Buddha. But, he also understood it to be our *shinjin*. In this sense, *shinjin* can be comprehended as the mind of pure aspiration, which arises in our hearts and minds.

Thus far, I have discussed the first two aspects of *shinjin*: deep mind and true mind. I have mentioned that deep mind is *shinjin* as seen from a psychological point of view, while true mind is *shinjin* as seen from a philosophical point of view. In keeping with that approach, when we discuss the issue of how we can live as human beings, *shinjin* may be looked upon as the mind of aspiration. That is, the mind of aspiration is *shinjin* seen from an ethical perspective.

Shin Buddhism has long been concerned about the actions or behavior of persons who are living in *shinjin*. It is believed that each person living in *shinjin* has his or her own path to follow. Shinran, for instance, comments on the way of life of the person of the *nembutsu* by saying that one who commits karmic evil shows no "signs" of *shinjin*. He also says that one who performs good acts manifests "signs" of *shinjin*. Here, "signs" has the meaning of "marks," "indications," or "proof." Thus, for Shinran, a life of *shinjin* manifests itself in apparent marks, gives rise to indications, and provides clear proof that one is living in *shinjin* in daily life. In other words, each person who is living in true *shinjin* manifests her or his own signs as definite proof.

Aspiring for Buddhahood To Save Sentient Beings

This means that we will inevitably come to follow ways of life in society that are appropriate to *shinjin*. What does this signify in concrete terms? Shinran explains that *shinjin* is true mind and pure mind. The nature of pure mind is that of self-benefit, in which we live according to the fundamental principles that pervade the world of humanity and the universe. The character of true mind is that of benefiting others, in which we embrace all other living beings in order to enable them to enter the realm of truth. Shinran adopts the language of T'an-luan to further clarify the pure mind of self-benefit and the true mind of benefiting others, calling them, respectively, the "mind that aspires for Buddhahood" and the "mind to save sentient beings."

In Shinran's words, the mind that aspires for Buddhahood is "deeply entrusting oneself to Amida's compassionate Vow and aspiring to become Buddha." The mind to save sentient beings is "the mind that desires to bring all sentient beings to Buddhahood."[20] In other words, living in *shinjin* means basically that we learn the Buddha-dharma and say the *nembutsu*, wishing to attain Buddhahood ourselves; further, we engage in action for the sake of all other persons and all living beings in order to allow them to realize true happiness. The fervent aim of our lives are both our own attainment of Buddhahood and the attainment of enlightenment by all others.

Thus, in Shin Buddhism living in *shinjin* means that we seek true happiness in life for ourselves and at the same time we aspire to bring all beings to the attainment of true happiness. Moreover, acts of self-benefit (for one's own Buddhahood) and acts of benefiting others (so that they may attain Buddhahood) must not be taken to be separate matters. Rather, the two must always be fulfilled as one. The Mahayana principle of compassionate action assumes this inseparability as its basic stance. This also forms the fundamental principle of ethics in Shin Buddhism. Shin Buddhist ethics and social action that is based on *shinjin* refer to the actions that we engage in when our aspiration for Buddhahood is identical to our wish to save sentient beings. Inevitably, as we walk our own paths to enlightenment we will come to engage in action for the sake of our neighbors and, more broadly, for the sake of society as a whole. I would like to consider some of the concrete implications of this in the next chapter, "Shin Buddhist Life."

NOTES

1   Please refer to the Translator's Notes for a discussion of

the word *shin*.
2   Nagarjuna, *The Commentary on the Ten Bodhisattva Stages* (Skt. Daśabhūmika-vibhāsā-śāstra, Jpn. Jūjū Bibasharon), cited in CWS, 24.
3   *Hymns of the Pure Land* (*Jōdo Wasan*), #115; in CWS, 357.
4   *Sutra of the Samadhi of Heroic Advance* (Skt. *Śūramgama-samādhi Sutra*, Jpn. *Shuryōgongyō*), cited in CWS, 497.
5   *Notes on the Inscriptions on Sacred Scrolls* (*Songō shinzō meimon*), in CWS, 498.
6   Hajime Nakamura, *Ways of Thinking of Eastern Peoples: India—China—Tibet—Japan*, trans. & ed. Philip P. Wiener (Honolulu: University of Hawaii Press, 1964).
7   *Hymns of the Dharma-Ages* (*Shōzōmatsu Wasan*), #34 & 35, in CWS, 407.
8   *Notes on Once-Calling and Many-Calling* (*Ichinen tanen mon'i*), in CWS, 454-455.
9   *Hymns of the Dharma-Ages*, in CWS, 407.
10   *A Record in Lament of Divergences*, 2, in CWS, 662.
11   Nishida Kitaro, *Bashōteki Ronri to Shūkyōteki Sekaikan* (The Logic of Place and the Religious Worldview) (Tokyo: Iwanami Shoten, 1966).
12   This rephrasing of the Eighteenth Vow and the passage on the fulfillment of the Eighteenth Vow has been done to capture the essential purport of the Vow.
13   *Notes on 'Essentials of Faith Alone'* (*Yuishinshō mon'i*), in CWS, 463.
14   Shan-tao, *Commentary on the Contemplation Sutra*

Shinjin

(*Kangyōshō*), chap. "On Nonmeditative Practice," cited in CWS, 85.
15 *A Record in Lament of Divergences*, 6, in CWS, 664.
16 *Notes on 'Essentials of Faith Alone,'* in CWS, 453.
17 *Hymns on the Pure Land Masters* (*Kōsō wasan*), in CWS, 371.
18 *Gutoku's Notes* (*Gutokushō*), in CWS, 594.
19 Cited in *True Teaching, Practice, and Realization*, in CWS, 80.
20 *Hymns of the Dharma-Ages*, #20 & notes, in CWS, 404.

Part Three

Shin Buddhist Life

Chapter One

Salvation in Shin Buddhism

Types of Religious Salvation

What does living in *shinjin* really mean? We will now take up this question in connection with three related topics: (1) the structure of salvation in *shinjin*, (2) the actual nature of salvation, and (3) the way of life of the Shin Buddhist follower. In other words, we will consider what being "saved by Amida Buddha" signifies in Shin Buddhism. Before we do, however, I would first like to look at some ways in which salvation is addressed in religions generally.

Schopenhauer's Theory of Happiness

In order for us to understand this topic, it would help if we first became acquainted with a theory of happiness that was offered by the German philosopher Arthur Schopenhauer (1788-1860). According to this theory, happiness or fulfillment in human life is always a relative thing, for it depends upon the relationship between what a person desires and what a person possesses. That is, Schopenhauer says that the degree of a person's happiness or fulfillment is like a fraction, in which one's desires serve as the denominator and one's possessions form the numerator. For instance, say that a person now possesses one hundred dollars. If that person should desire to have one thousand dollars, that person's degree of fulfillment would be just ten percent. If, however, that person only wanted to have fifty dollars, his degree of fulfillment would be two hundred percent. In other words, the resultant fraction cannot be obtained simply from the fact that one possesses one hundred dollars. The degree of happiness or fulfillment in human life is always relative, for it is determined by the relationship between our desires and our possessions.

Three Ways of Seeking Happiness

Now let us consider three ways in which we seek

happiness in human life. I should note that this is entirely my own idea, although it is based on Schopenhauer's thinking.

What, then, is the first way of seeking happiness? Happiness in human life is the result of a fractional computation, in which the denominator represents our desires and the numerator our possessions. Our desires constantly grow in number throughout our lives. Thus, we spend our lives constantly worrying that our possessions (the numerator) are too few and small, compared to our desires (the denominator). In order for us to be happy, we think, our numerators need to grow, and so we are constantly obsessed with increasing the amount and size of our possessions. In this scheme, we feel that life is going well for us whenever our fraction has a value greater than one, that is, when our possessions outnumber our desires. When that happens, we think, we are able to enjoy fulfillment and happiness. It follows, then, that the first way to seek happiness is simply to strive mightily to increase the amount of our possessions. Simply put, the reason that many of us are now working at our jobs is simply to add to our numerators. This is the first way of seeking happiness.

The second method of seeking happiness uses the same fractional computation to determine the degree of our fulfillment and happiness. Here, however, we use any means available to lessen the amount of our desires, so that our denominators will be smaller than our numerators. If we are able to make our resultant fractions greater than one, we feel that we will be able to enjoy lives of fulfillment. In other words, the second method of seeking happiness is to seek fulfillment by trying to bring our wants and needs under control. The problem is that our human wants and needs are constantly growing without end. Hence, this method of pursuing happiness relies upon our human ingenuity, which is only sometimes effective.

We have now considered two ways of seeking happiness in life: the first increases our possessions, while the second lessens our desires. However, in life we are usually unable either to add to our numerators or subtract from our denominators. As a result, the value of our happiness is going to be a fraction that is less than one. What, then, are we to do? It is at such times that we can discover a third way of seeking happiness. It is here, where the results are harsh and our fractions are considerably less than one, that a new formula can come into play—a method that can lead to a value that will always be greater than one. We then can possess an unshakeable attitude toward human life, one that will enable us to overcome all of life's sufferings and sorrows. What is attainable here is another kind of human life.

I have presented you with my own theory of human happiness, which takes a hint from Schopenhauer's thought.

The third way of seeking happiness is the most important one, I believe. Therefore, I will describe it more fully as I discuss three general types of religious salvation, which correspond to these three ways of seeking happiness.

Salvation as the Fulfillment of Desire

Supernatural Power

The first type of salvation in religion might be called "salvation as the fulfillment of desire," for it corresponds to the first method of seeking happiness that we saw above. Here, the attainment of happiness is said to result when we increase the number of our possessions. This basically implies that what will save us in the end will be human resourcefulness and ability alone. The problem is that there will be times in our lives when, for instance, our businesses are not successful in spite of all of our hard work. Or, there will be occasions when we have an illness that is incurable even though we may receive all possible treatment. That is to say, there will be times when our possessions (our numerators) do not increase as we think they should, no matter how much we try to add to them.

At times like this, many of us will resort to a variety of measures. Some of us may pick ourselves up from defeat and try again. Others may seek the help of others. And yet, more often than not, the amount of our possessions and the situations in which we find ourselves will not measure up to our needs or wishes. In our suffering and distress, many of us may pray to gods for help. We may accept the existence of some kind of supernatural or divine power, and pray in supplication to the gods in order to enlist the aid of that power. Many of us will attempt in this way to improve upon our possessions, so that they may measure up to our hopes and wishes. This is what some religions refer to as being "saved." Such religions assert that salvation takes place when the circumstances of our lives are improved so that they equal the level of our wants and desires, through the power of gods or supernatural powers.

Petitionary Prayers and Miracles

Religions that espouse this kind of salvation presume the existence of a supernatural power, which rules over this world and all human life. Many of those religions speak about the existence of a transcendent, supernatural being, which many name "God." All phenomena in the world, they say, occur as a result of the will of that transcendent, supernatural being. Such religions also teach that every human life is controlled by that same power.

This, for example, is what the traditional Japanese religion of Shintō teaches. Shintō is a polytheistic religion.

Each of its many gods, or *kami*, is assigned its own allotted responsibility within the overall scheme of the world and human life. The many *kami*, it is said, correspond to a range of human desires. Hence, just as there are *kami* of the mountains, seas, wind, and rain, there are also *kami* for making money, meeting one's mate, entering college, traffic safety, and other events. Each *kami*, it is said, responds to the human wish that it is responsible for.

In order to benefit from the power of the *kami* it is necessary for humans to petition in prayer to them. Above all else, people must confess their own desires and pray fervently to the *kami* with all of their might in order to obtain salvation from the *kami*. When those prayers are effectively communicated to the *kami*, what can occur is a miracle that surpasses all human conception. As a result, the circumstances of people's lives (their numerators) become manifest in ways exactly as they had desired. In this kind of religion, such a phenomenon is considered to be "salvation." We can see this today in the teaching of Shintō.

Of course, some question whether the Japanese people of today actually believe in the power and miracles of the *kami*, and to what extent they do. Yet, even now throngs of people still go to worship at the well-known shrines. It is said that during special Japanese holidays, such as the New Year celebrations, over eighty million people (more than two-thirds of the entire population of Japan) go to Shintō shrines to worship and pray. It would appear that, even in modern-day Japan, many still believe in this kind of religious salvation.

In various other places in the world today, there are a great number of religions that also espouse this kind of salvation. They even exist in contemporary societies that boast highly developed scientific and technological cultures. Often, when people meet with unforeseen misfortune and come face-to-face with irresolvable trouble, they turn completely away from their usual ways of thinking and attitudes toward life, and they cast their lot with irrational religious claims. There are more than a few of us who seek after this kind of salvation.

This type of salvation can be seen primarily in primitive religions and ancient societies. Yet, even today many religions continue to carry on those primitive traditions. In addition, we have recently observed the growth of various religions of the occult, which clothe themselves in scientific guise. They talk about healing the sufferings and afflictions of human life, and make spurious claims that persons can attain superpowers by engaging in certain practices and austerities. When it comes down to it, however, all religions that offer this kind of salvation are actually just affirming human desires and are seeking to fulfill those desires by appealing to some supernatural power. Religions of this type tend to focus on the attainment of benefits in the

Shin Buddhist Life

present life.

Salvation through Self-Control

Will of a Transcendent, Absolute Being

The second type of religious salvation might be called "salvation gained through self-control." This corresponds to the second way of seeking happiness, which we saw above, in which we try to realize happiness in our lives by reducing the amount of our desires.

Our efforts to control or lessen our desires rely primarily on calculations made by our human resourcefulness and ingenuity. Often, our lives do not go as we think they should. When we find that our wishes are not being realized, we put to work an array of our own cleverness and resourcefulness in order to cut back on those wishes, if ever slightly. We may, for instance, modify our original objectives and go with plan B or plan C, or we may simply forgo those goals altogether and replace them with new wishes.

We believe that, by rethinking our original paths and setting out on paths that are entirely new, we are likely to discover happiness greater than we had known before. This is the goal of human life. The problem is that we human beings are not able to control our own desires very well.

Many of us are more apt to stick to our original wants or wishes until the bitter end, eventually falling away from our personal paths and bringing ruin upon ourselves.

This type of salvation differs from salvation as the fulfillment of desires, which we looked at earlier. In the first type of salvation, human desires are affirmed even as we pursue the fulfillment or satisfaction of those desires. Here, in contrast, we focus on the problem of our own desires and wants, and seek to bring them under control.

This kind of religion also establishes, first and foremost, the existence of a transcendent, absolute deity, which created and now rules over everything in this world and human life. We human beings, it is taught, should simply place our faith in that absolute deity and live in obedience to His will, for the will of that absolute being constantly manifests itself in the realities of this world and human life. Hence, if our lives are not going according to our wishes or even going contrary to our desires, it is all due to the will of God, and we should thus accept this current state of reality just as it is.

In other words, we seek to bring ourselves into accord with the realities of life by bringing our own wishes and desires under control. In this way, the amount of desires in our denominators is reduced quite nicely. We come to accept the realities of our existence, even while the amount of our possessions in our numerators remains unchanged.

Shin Buddhist Life

The resultant fractional value is thus greater than one. Hence, even though the circumstances of our lives remain unchanged, we are able, perhaps, to experience happiness and fulfillment. This is the notion of salvation through self-control.

Faith and Self-Modification

Religions that espouse this kind of salvation also presume the existence of a transcendent, absolute being that controls this world and human life. They speak of the need to have complete obedience to that being and absolute submission to that God's will.

For example, I believe that we can see this tendency in the teachings of Tenrikyō, a Japanese folk religion, which was founded by Nakayama Miki (1798-1887) at around the time of the Meiji Restoration. Today its devotees number as many as 1,800,000 persons, including those living outside of Japan. Tenrikyō speaks of a transcendent *kami* named Tenri-Ō-no-mikoto. This *kami*, it is taught, is absolute; it created the universe and rules over all of the creatures within it.

Tenrikyō teaches that true human happiness is brought about when people live in obedience to the will of that kami. That *kami* is referred as "hōki" (literally, "broom"). People who have faith in that *kami* are able to sweep away their own self-centered thoughts and live solely in accordance with the mind of that *kami*. Their own self-centered minds are referred to as "*hokori*" (literally, "dust motes"), for they are said to contain eight kinds of dust: miserliness, desire, hatred, self-love, malice, anger, greed, and arrogance.

Devotees utter these words of prayer: "O Tenri-Ō-no-mikoto! I pray that you will sweep away this evilness and save me!" In so doing, they are able to accept the conditions of their lives and find fulfillment in them, as they fervently sweep away or purify their minds of dust and thereby bring their desires and wants under control. By gaining this kind of self-control, it is taught, people will be able to live joyful lives.

This type of religion, which emphasizes self-control or self-modification based on faith, can often be seen in the new Japanese religions of today. However, we need to exercise caution with this kind of religion, for when it draws too close to political authority and affixes itself to the political establishment, it starts to work in such a way that makes the masses submit in obeisance to those authorities. Karl Marx (1818-1883) criticized religion for being an opiate of the masses, and indeed there is the danger that this kind of religion may perform that role.

Shin Buddhist Life

Salvation as the Establishment of Personal Subjectivity

Basic Principles of the World and Human Beings

A third type of salvation corresponds to the third way of seeking happiness, which I will now explain in more detail. Here, even though the value of our fractions of human happiness may be less than one, a new formula can come into play in which the result will always be greater than one. In other words, happiness can result when we are able to establish a new stance toward human life each and every day. Here, "greater than one" means that each of us can develop a fundamentally new attitude toward human life and commence on a new way of living as a human being. Establishing this kind of stance is not simply a matter of changing our minds or shifting our thinking. Rather, it is a reformation—a growth of our humanity—which takes place at the level of our own subjectivity, the deepest level at which human life operates. We may call this type of salvation "salvation as the establishment of our personal subjectivity."

Many religions teach of this kind of reformation or growth of our humanity. However, I believe it is most clearly visible in the Buddhist path of enlightenment. As I mentioned earlier, the fundamental principle of the

Buddhist teaching reveals a path of awakening leading to the attainment of enlightenment. Our lives on that path are situated at the point of intersection of the vertical axis of self—responsibility and the horizontal axis of the universal dharmic-principle. On that path we are all enabled to grow into the kinds of persons that we are capable of becoming—that is, we become transformed into human beings in the truest sense.

We have also seen that the Buddhist teachings can be divided into those centered on renunciant monks and those focusing on lay householders. The Path of Sages, or Buddhism for renunciants, emphasizes the ultimate truth of enlightenment (*satori*) and the experience of awakening as the fundamental principle that pervades this world and all human life. In contrast, Pure Land Buddhism, which is the path for householders, speaks of the experience of awakening to or "truly knowing" Amida Buddha, the symbol of that fundamental principle and ultimate truth. Both forms of Buddhism teach us about the importance of practice, which needs to be performed in order to realize that experience and which then coincides with that experience. The Path of Sages expounds many forms of practice from various standpoints. The Pure Land teaching focuses on the practice of saying the *nembutsu*, which is based solely on the path of aspiring for enlightenment and hearing the Dharma.

Shin Buddhist Life

We have also seen that the experience of awakening, which we realize through the practice of the *nembutsu*, inevitably brings us to cast off our old selves and nurture the growth of a new personal human subjectivity. Where this kind of personal subjectivity is established we come to realize paths upon which we are able to overcome the many hardships and obstructions that exist in the current situations of our lives.

In Buddhism the fundamental expression for "being saved" involves the idea of being able to "cross over" (*saido*). The Sanskrit word that corresponds to this notion of "crossing over" is *uttarana*, the original meaning of which is to "traverse, go across, or pass over." It means that one transcends or crosses over many and varied obstructions. The Chinese character *sai* (済) indicates that one crosses over a body of water, while *do* (度) means that one traverses across various obstacles or hindrances.

Thus, salvation in Buddhism and Shin Buddhism is clearly different from either of the two types of salvation that we discussed earlier. It is completely unlike "salvation as the fulfillment of desires." There, the afflictions present in one's current state of existence are altered to conform to one's own desires and wishes, through prayer asking for the intervention of an absolute being. It also differs from "salvation through self-control." There, the contradictions and difficulties present in one's current state of being are resolved by modifying one's own thoughts, desires, and wants through faith in an absolute being. In stark contrast to these types of salvation in Buddhism means that we become subjectively able to cross over our current situation (even though it is still our current situation) and overcome our afflictions (even as they remain our afflictions), as we establish our own personal growth and subjectivity.

"Birth" in the Pure Land teachings represents the most direct and straightforward symbol of this path of "crossing over" and "overcoming." For human beings, the most difficult event to cross over and overcome is death. When we come face-to-face with death, in that moment, everything that we had cherished in life, such as status, wealth, and love, becomes useless and valueless. All human beings are born into this world naked, alone, and possessed of nothing, and so we must also die naked and alone, bearing nothing at all.

However, Pure Land Buddhism teaches that when we have realized a change in our humanity and established a new personal subjectivity in the *nembutsu* and *shinjin* we are able to traverse across all of the afflictions of life and transcend—that is, cross over—even death itself. Death is not the end of everything. Instead, it becomes the beginning —the birth—of a new and authentic human life. In this sense, in the Pure Land teachings, death means that one is born anew. One "goes to be born" (*ōjō*, 往生). Salvation in

Buddhism, and particularly in Pure Land Buddhism, is described most clearly through the symbol of birth.

Still, birth does not simply mean that we go to be reborn in the Pure Land after we have died. Rather, birth signifies the life of one who has realized true *shinjin*, which is the experience of awakening. It refers to the life of one who has been saved by Amida Buddha. No matter how terrible the difficulties and afflictions that we may encounter, when we say the *nembutsu* earnestly, we are continuously crossing over them, one sure step at a time. This is the meaning of "birth."

Establishment of a New Personal Subjectivity

Thus, the Buddhist teaching directs us toward the experience of awakening to the fundamental principle, or dharma, which pervades this world and our lives. One who realizes this experience is "saved." Salvation in the Path of Sages and salvation in the Pure Land Path refer to the same, fundamental experience. Both teach that a person can establish a new personal subjectivity within the experience of awakening, and thereby cross over and overcome all of the many afflictions and obstructions present in the current state of one's human life.

Here is an example of salvation in the Path of Sages. Long ago, there was a Rinzai Zen priest by the name of

Kaisen (d. 1582), who was the high priest of Erin-ji temple in Yamanashi prefecture. Erin-ji had gotten caught up in a dispute between some regional warlords. As a result, it was attacked and set on fire. Kaisen, as the resident priest of the temple, felt deeply responsible for this turn of events. Because of that he climbed to the upper balcony of the temple gate and sat in the middle of the fire, which was blazing in rolling flames. There he composed a death poem, which stated,

> Sitting quietly at peace,
> I have no need of mountain streams;
> When thoughts of the mind are quelled,
> Even the flames are cool.

He then died serenely. It is likely that Kaisen was able to look into the face of death in this remarkable way because he had already established a strong personal subjectivity during his life. This an example of a superb way of living in the face of death by one who had lived intently in the Path of Sages, the path of enlightenment for renunciant monks.

Another person who lived on the same Path of Sages was Ryōkan (1758-1831), a Sōtō Zen priest who lived in Niigata prefecture. The following story has been told about him. The area in which Ryōkan lived had been struck by a huge earthquake and many people had perished. It was at

Shin Buddhist Life

that time that someone asked Ryōkan how one might be able to escape from such terrible disasters. In response, Ryōkan sent him a letter, which stated,

> When you meet with disaster, you should truly meet it. When it is time to die, you should truly die. This is the wondrous teaching that will enable you to escape disaster.

When disaster strikes, one should accept the fact that disaster has struck. When death arrives, one should accept the reality of death. That is, no matter what disaster one might encounter, one should accept it subjectively, taking it personally into oneself. In that way, one will truly be able to transcend it and cross over it. I think that we can appreciate the way of life of Ryōkan, who had established a wondrous, personal subjectivity through arduous religious practice.

Among past Shin Buddhist householders, whose paths of enlightenment were based on the teachings of Shinran and the *nembutsu*, we can find many who also established a new personal subjectivity and lived excellent lives. One such person was Hōrin (1693-1741). A Shin Buddhist priest, he was also the fourth Nōke of Nishi-Hongwanji's Gakurin (a position equivalent to the President of the current Ryūkoku University). Hōrin lived in deep *shinjin*, and thus he was sharply critical of the secularization not only within the religious institutions of his time, but within himself as well. He left the following poem, which he wrote at the time of his death:

> The single way to birth is settled during ordinary life.
> That I speak today not of death and birth
> Is not because I long for the bliss of the lotus world,
> For I will return to this saha world to teach and save sentient beings.

Hōrin is saying that the problem of his death has already been resolved during his life. Hence, he will not now speak of birth and death, for he will go to be born in the Pure Land. However, he does not long for the pleasures of the Pure Land in any way. Rather, he will immediately come back to this world as one who directs virtue in the aspect of return, and will lead other beings to birth as well. A look at Hōrin's actual text reveals that his penmanship in the latter half of this passage becomes very messy and unclear, making it barely legible. It is said that he wrote this passage just as his life was coming to an end. Long ago I had the opportunity to read Hōrin's original text. When I came upon this deathbed poem, I felt strongly that he was a person who lived, and died, in true *shinjin*.

Another Shin Buddhist follower was Ashikaga Genza

(1842-1930) who lived in Tottori prefecture. Even though Genza experienced many troubles in his life, he lived exclusively in the *nembutsu* and deeply in *shinjin*. One of Genza's friends was a person by the name of Naoji. As he grew older and came to face the immediacy of his own death, Naoji began to study the Buddha-dharma seriously every day with Genza. Finally, it was time for him to die. Yet, many doubts and thoughts of anxiety filled his mind. "I just can't die like this!" he thought, and so he had his granddaughter deliver a message to Genza in which he complained about his distress and asked Genza to teach him what to do. At that moment, however, Genza himself was also on his deathbed. When Genza heard the message about Naoji's inner turmoil, he had the granddaughter deliver this response to his friend: "Naoji! It's okay to die, just as you are." Upon saying these words, Genza then passed away.

When we open our eyes of *shinjin*, we find that we are now—and we already have been—embraced within the arms of the Buddha. However, if we have not yet realized *shinjin*—if we have not deeply understood, or awakened to, or been able to experience its reality—then we will be afraid and feel that we cannot die in such a state. However, when we deeply awaken to and experience the reality of *shinjin*, then no matter when or where, and however terribly death might call upon us, we will know that "it's okay to die, just as we are."

An ancient poem states,

> Wherever the snail dies—
> That is its home!

A snail goes through life always carrying its own home on its back. Hence, wherever it may die, it will be inside its own home, and thus it will be able to die with peace of mind. This is exactly what Ryōkan meant when he said, "When it is time to die, you should truly die." Here as well we can see the way of living—and the way of dying—in deep *shinjin*, and we can observe the image of one who is able to cross over and transcend death. This is the true Buddhist way of life of one who has realized the experience of awakening and established a new personal subjectivity, and thus has been saved.

Above, I have classified religious salvation broadly into three types, and explained each by citing some concrete religious examples. I have described them by emphasizing each of their distinguishing features. In many religions these three types of salvation overlap with one another in a variety of ways. Moreover, even in the same religion these types of salvation may sometimes vary, depending on the depth or shallowness of an individual's own faith. Therefore, it is impossible to make a simple classification of types of religious salvation. Still, here I have sought to make a broad classification of them, based on the respective differences in their character.

Shinjin and Human Life

The Ethics of *Shinjin*

Shinjin and Society

Today, many of the traditional authorities and values that we once held are crumbling. As a result, it is becoming very difficult for us to discern our true path in life. I feel this acutely every time some horrific incident, which is altogether impossible to understand through common sense, is reported in the news. I believe that any society of human beings, of any era and in any place, has to be grounded in rules that tell us what absolutely cannot be done or what must be minimally obeyed. In other words, there are certain universal systems of human ethics or rules that we must follow. Yet, does it not seem, in today's society, that such ethical systems and rules are gradually being lost?

The need for social order will naturally arise as long as humans exist, for people must properly abide by it in order for them to live together. At the same time, however, each and every human being possesses basic individual rights and liberties that cannot be overlooked. And if people are to live fully, then these must be valued to the highest extent possible. Yet, in today's society it seems as though there is a split between social order and rules on the one hand and individual rights and liberties on the other. And, it seems as though we are losing a sense of balance between the two. More and more of us, it seems, are bent on leading self-centered lives. We appear to have forgotten that individual rights, not to mention individual dignity and freedom, can be truly guaranteed only when social order and rules are sufficiently upheld as well.

I believe that an ideal society is formed when order and rules, which represent societal authority, and individual rights and liberties are in correspondence and are effectively integrated with one another. I also believe that, in order to create such a society, it would be extremely important for all individuals, from a very early age, to learn those universal values and truths essential to our humanness at the innermost depths of our personal consciousness. And, it would be equally vital that we continue to hold those values throughout our lives. I think that religion, more than anything else, has a significant role to play in endowing persons with those universal human values and in nurturing this kind of individual human growth.

In Shin Buddhism, the same thing can be said about *shinjin*, for, to the extent that it entails an individual's growth as a human being, *shinjin* will naturally require that we grapple with the societal nature of human life. We must ask the question: "How is a person living in *shinjin* to live within the realities of today's society?" However, according to the traditional interpretations of Shin Buddhist doctrine in the past and even currently, human beings will forever be possessed of defiled passions; our karmic evil will always be deep and profound, whether we have realized *shinjin* or not. Hence, it is said, we will never be able to change or improve ourselves, or perform any sort of good act. Throughout our lives we can do nothing but commit evil offenses over and over again, and thus amass nothing but karmic evil. Thus, we are told that we must desire solely to be born in the Pure Land in the life-to-come, after death. Such interpretations of *shinjin* completely evade the question of how we are to live with others in society. Such traditional thinking is represented in Rennyo's statement that "birth [in the Pure Land] is an individual accomplishment."[1]

However, is *shinjin* really like that? My position is that that is an overly conceptualized interpretation of *shinjin*, which presumes upon the great compassion of Amida Buddha. Thus, it reflects a misunderstanding of Shinran's thought. If I may repeat what I stated before, *shinjin* in Shin Buddhism is unquestionably an experience of awakening. This clearly means that it involves a transformation of our very personhood. It means that, as human beings, we cast off the skin of our old selves, little by little, as we are nurtured to become our new selves and realize true growth as human beings. Furthermore, *shinjin* is also the mind that aspires for Buddhahood and the mind to save sentient beings. At the same time as we realize our own growth as human beings, we also put forth our own efforts so that others may also realize such growth. *Shinjin* has both the character of self-benefit and of benefiting others at the same time. This inevitably forms the societal nature of *shinjin*, as we seek to shoulder the great task of somehow engaging with and responding appropriately to the various phenomena that envelop us within the realities of today's society.

Ultimate Truth and Worldly Truth

How, then, might *shinjin* properly engage with and

respond to the order and norms present in today's secular society? The traditional notion of *shinjin*'s relationship with society was developed shortly after Shinran's death by Zonkaku (1290-1373), the eldest son of Kakunyo, who was the third head priest of the Hongwanji. Zonkaku described the relationship between the Buddha-dharma (ultimate truth) and imperial laws (worldly truth) to be the same as that between the two wheels of a cart or two wings of a bird. His position was that these two forms of law always depend upon and support one another. The problem is that, in such a relationship, the Buddha-dharma, or *shinjin*, will inevitably be made subordinate to worldly laws and secular authorities. And, in actual fact, for many years after, the Hongwanji organization became largely controlled by and subordinate to the ruling authorities and political system of Japan.

Rennyo, the eighth head priest of the Hongwanji, later held that Shin Buddhist followers should "take *shinjin* as primary" on the one hand, even as they "make imperial law primary; and make humanity and justice foremost" on the other.[2] He taught that people ought to distinguish clearly between the Buddha-dharma (*shinjin*) and secular laws and authorities (including societal ethics). Not only that, people should focus their lives on either or both dimensions, depending upon the situation. Clearly, Rennyo dualistically separated *shinjin* from worldly authorities and ethics. And yet, he also spoke of the mutual dependence between such completely different dimensions. Rennyo's influence on Shin Buddhist thought has been great and, following him, this dualist separation between *shinjin* and secular life long existed.

However, with the Meiji Restoration, Japan began to undertake new interchange with other countries. As it absorbed much of European culture, in particular, Japanese society itself became quite diversified. As a consequence, the relationship between *shinjin* in Shin Buddhism and societal life became even more complex, and the relationship between the two once again became the focus of inquiry. It was at that time that a new doctrinal theme arose in Shin Buddhism that was referred to as "the two truths: ultimate and worldly" (*shinzoku nitairon*). Here, "ultimate truth" was a reference to the truth of the Buddha-dharma or the principle of *shinjin*. "Worldly truth" referred to the social order or secular principles. In other words, "the two truths: ultimate and worldly" represented an attempt to examine the relationship between the ultimate truth of *shinjin* and the worldly principles of secular society. Shin Buddhist studies of the late nineteenth and early twentieth centuries offered a great range of scholarly theories regarding this theme.

I believe that we can group such approaches to "the two truths: ultimate and worldly" into five broad categories.

They are: (1) ultimate and worldly truths are a single truth, (2) ultimate and worldly are parallel truths, (3) ultimate and worldly are interrelated truths, (4) ultimate truth influences worldly truth, and (5) worldly truth is a means to realize ultimate truth.

The first category, that ultimate and worldly truths are a single truth, contains two sub-theories: (a) ultimate truth is the single truth, and (b) worldly truth is the single truth. The theory that ultimate truth is a single truth very clearly espouses a way of life that is based solely on the Buddha-dharma or *shinjin*. Here, ultimate truth means that, aside from the Buddha-dharma, no standard of value exists in human social life. This position urges all Shin Buddhist followers to live according to the principles of the Buddha-dharma or *shinjin*. In contrast, the theory that worldly truth is the single truth takes the position that the principles of secular society and their ethical values overlie the principles of the Buddha-dharma and *shinjin*. Hence, this approach urges Shin Buddhists to live in accordance with the worldly principles and the ethical values upon which the social order is based.

The second category, that ultimate and worldly are parallel truths, considers the principle of *shinjin* (ultimate truth) and the principles of society (worldly truth) to be of completely different natures. The two, it is said, arise separately, each having no relationship to the other.

The third category, that ultimate and worldly are interrelated truths, coincides with the ideas of Zonkaku and Rennyo, which we saw earlier. The Buddha-dharma (ultimate truth) and imperial law or societal norms (worldly truth) are interrelated and mutually dependent on each other. It is claimed that the principle of the Buddha-dharma supports the principles of imperial law and society; at the same time, the principles of imperial law and society sustain the principle of the Buddha-dharma.

The thinking reflected by the fourth category, that ultimate truth influences worldly truth, is that the Buddha-dharma and *shinjin* influence secular society and societal life unilaterally. That is, ultimate truth moves in the direction of worldly truth. Here also there are two sub-theories. In the first, the principle of the Buddha-dharma and *shinjin* (ultimate truth) flows directly, and develops unchanged, into societal principles and societal life. The second theory is that ultimate truth will always exert its influence on worldly truth by taking form in an indirect way.

Finally, the fifth category, that worldly truth is a means to realize ultimate truth, takes the position that societal principles and social life (worldly truth) act as expedient means for the arising and deepening of *shinjin* (ultimate truth). This theory also contains two sub-theories. The first holds that worldly truth is an affirmative means to the realization of ultimate truth. In other words, the perfection of our societal lives (worldly truth) will directly bring about the arising of *shinjin*. The second theory is that worldly truth is a negative means to realize ultimate truth. According to this notion, human beings are completely unable to eliminate evil or perform good acts in this worldly life (worldly truth). Thus, it is said, only the total breakdown of ethics and morals in society, and our reflection upon it, will enable humans to turn to and enter the world of *shinjin*.

Even to this day, the world of Shin Buddhist studies is split up according to the way that scholars and their theories regard the two truths: ultimate and worldly.

Living in *Shinjin*

We have had an overview of some of the traditional scholarly theories regarding the relationship between *shinjin* and social life in Shin Buddhism. However, we must now ask ourselves: "Could any of these approaches direct us to a life of *shinjin* that would be in accord with Shinran's true intent?" I would answer that the very first of the theories could do so. That is, I believe that the idea that ultimate truth is the single truth reveals the true manner in which *shinjin* is connected to societal life.

Among Shin Buddhists of the past, Shichiri Gojun was

the only person to set forth the notion that the ultimate and worldly truths are a single truth. I believe that we can learn much from studying his thought. According to Shichiri, ultimate truth signifies that we discard all things of this world and aspire for birth in the Pure Land. Worldly truth means that we expend all of our energies for the sake of the world. He asserted sternly that, within the societal lives of Shin Buddhist followers, we need first of all to completely reject this secular world in our experience of *shinjin* (ultimate truth). For it is only when we discard all aspects of this secular world that, for the first time, an authentic worldly truth—a true societal life—will come about. The acts of rejecting the world and living in the world completely contradict each other. However, Shichiri said that the simultaneous occurrence of the two is an indication of the inconceivable Shin Buddhist experience of *shinjin*. It is exactly at this point that a true social life of a Shin Buddhist follower can be undertaken. I believe that we need to listen carefully and pay close attention to this kind of thinking.

Shichiri illustrated this idea with this simple example. "*Shinjin* is just like a millstone," he said. "It can have only one [center] shaft. If you try to use two shafts, then the millstone will not turn." In other words, human life cannot be based on two principles or two truths, such as the ultimate and the worldly. Life can only turn around one axle—the principle of *shinjin* or ultimate truth. He then offered these expressions: "When you speak, speak silently. When you run, run while seated." "This world is provided by the Tathagata. We should use it as if we were borrowing it from the Buddha." Shichiri sought to teach us that, when we earnestly say the *nembutsu*, that *nembutsu* serves as the axle that enables us to awaken to the truth that all things in this world and human life are without exception empty and false, totally without truth and sincerity. And yet, at the same time, we are also enabled to live to the utmost, for we come to value this world and human life (which are still empty, false, totally without truth or sincerity) as things borrowed from the Buddha.

Shichiri Gojun's expressions, I believe, are similar to the words of Shinran, "I am now neither monk nor one in worldly life" (*hisō hizoku*), in the concluding passages of his text True Teaching, Practice, and Realization.[3] Shinran used these words to describe how he was dispossessed of his priestly status during the movement to suppress the *nembutsu*. The expression itself originally appeared in the life story of Kyōshin (ca. eighth or ninth century C.E.) of Kago in Japan, whom Shinran revered as an early forerunner in the Pure Land way. I believe that the words "neither monk nor one in worldly life" express Shinran's fundamental attitude toward his own humanity, which permeated his entire life. If I were to apply this phrase to

Shin Buddhist Life

the theory of the two truths, ultimate and worldly, it might be rendered as "neither ultimate nor worldly."

What then would it mean to live in a way that is "neither ultimate nor worldly"? Our lives would not simply be both ultimate and worldly, or both worldly and ultimate. Nor would they be half—ultimate and half—worldly. Rather, we would live in a way that is neither ultimate nor worldly and neither worldly nor ultimate. That is to say, both dimensions of our lives would undergo self-negation. And yet, at the same time, they would become a single dimension, leading to the dawning of new horizons within our lives. We would ache with terrible pain over the fact that our daily lives are not ultimate or true—for we live contrary to the Buddha-dharma and are sunk deeply within the secular world. And yet, we would also live with profound aspiration when we realize that our daily lives are also not worldly—for we seek to live nearer to the Buddha-dharma and reject this secular world, little by little. Thus, "neither ultimate nor worldly" signifies a complex interplay between the pain of being not true and the wish not to be of the world.

This is the way of life that Shichiri Gojun described with the words "when you speak, speak silently. When you run, run while seated." To me, this refers to the world that arises for the first time when we live each and every day by saying the *nembutsu*. It is the path in which the ultimate is the single truth—a oneness of the ultimate and the worldly, in which these two contradictory truths are realized in paradoxical identity. That is to say, even though we are living in the midst of this secular world, we aspire earnestly for the Pure Land, the supramundane world, as we critically de-absolutize all things in this secular world as false and empty.

Therefore, in Shin Buddhism, to be engaged in society within *shinjin* means that each and every day our lives are grounded in a critical and relentless de-absolutization and negation of our own human lives and secular society. And, at the same time, our involvement in the world takes place within a complex interaction between—and identity of—profound pain and aspiration as to our own ways of living. I believe that the working of the mind that aspires for Buddhahood (self-benefit) and the mind to save sentient beings (benefiting others), which forms the inner reality of true and real *shinjin*, takes place in this kind of structure. It is an activity aimed toward our growth as human beings, as well as the development and maturation of all aspects of society. In this way, it represents the way in which Shin Buddhists can live authentically in the world.

The Starting Point for Understanding Buddhism

The Basic Commonality of All Life

Living in *shinjin* means that we are able to realize the experience of awakening for the first time in our lives. Upon awakening, we become deeply aware of the fact that the life of the Buddha reaches into our own lives, and that our lives gain connection with the life of the Buddha. And, we awaken to the reality that the Buddha's life is also connected expansively to the lives of all others—to all living beings other than ourselves. Our lives are defiled, for they are stained with ego-attachment and defiled passions. Even at this moment, we are living hellish lives. And yet, within the *nembutsu* and *shinjin*, the pure life of the Buddha is endlessly flowing into our lives of defiled passions. And, little by little, bit by bit, our lives, which are just like the utter darkness of hell, are transformed into the pure, brilliant life of the Pure Land. Shinran, as we have seen above, describes the structure of transformation in *shinjin* in this way.

> [E]vil karma, without being nullified or eradicated, is made into the highest good.[4]
> Obstructions of karmic evil turn into virtues;

> It is like the relation of ice and water:
> The more the ice, the more the water;
> The more the obstructions, the more the virtues.[5]

I have mentioned that the life of the Buddha is also connected with the lives of all other living beings. The word sattva, which we saw earlier, is an expression of this Buddhist perspective on life. The original meaning of the word was "being, existence, character, nature, and life." It was translated into Chinese as *shujō*, which refers to a being possessed of immeasurable lives or also a being that undergoes innumerable births and deaths. It was also translated as *ujō*, which indicates one that is capable of possessing many kinds of feelings. In other words, it refers to all things having life, including human beings, which exist in this world.

Hence, Buddhism teaches that all living beings possess a basic commonality with all other things. We are all fellow sentient beings in life. In the *Mahā Parinirvāṇa Sutra* it is taught that "all sentient beings have Buddhanature." That is, all living beings are possessed of the life of the Buddha. And, since all beings possess the life of the Buddha, we are all equal, for no kind of discrimination can exist within that life. This way of thinking differs clearly from many Western views of life. There it is taught that human beings alone join with the life of God, and are thus worthy of respect. All other beings have been provided by God for the sake of humans, and thus their lives are of lesser value.

The Buddhist perspective on life became more thoroughgoing in Chinese Buddhism. There, the idea developed that human life is connected, not just to other animal life, but also to all plants and trees. It was thought that a human life could be reborn, and become any variety of plant or tree, and that the life of a plant or tree could be reborn and become a human being. In Japan this Buddhist conception merged with ancient Japanese thinking. Hence, there developed the notion that the life of a human being has a basic commonality, not just with the lives of plants, but also with the land, rocks, and earth. This perspective on life predated views concerning the origin of life that are now endorsed by contemporary biological science.

The Teaching "Not to Kill"

The characteristic feature of the Buddhist perspective on life is that it teaches that all living things—and all life—are equal and connected to all other lives. Furthermore, it teaches that such life is to be valued, since all life shares in the life of the Buddha. It follows that Buddhism also teaches that the taking of the life of a living being is the gravest act of karmic evil that one can commit. According to an early Buddhist scripture, the *Sutta-nipata*, which, it is said, effectively transmits the original form of the words of Gautama Buddha,

> He should not kill a living being, nor cause it to be killed, nor should he incite another to kill. Do not injure any being, either strong or weak, in the world.[6]

Here, the Buddha instructs his followers not to take the life of any living being, not to make another person to take a life, and not to tolerate the taking of a life by another person.

From its earliest period, Buddhism promulgated five kinds of precepts for lay believers to follow. These five precepts are: (1) not to kill, (2) not to steal, (3) not to commit adultery, (4) not to tell lies, and (5) not to take intoxicants. Followers were severely cautioned against committing the five evil acts of violating these precepts. Here we can see that the first rule of life for a person learning the Buddhist teachings is the precept not to kill—not to take the life of a living being. Violating this precept is considered to be the first kind of karmic evil, and it can thus be said that the precept not to kill represents the starting point of Buddhist ethics. This precept is also seen in the Pure Land teachings of Amida Buddha, when, for instance, the *Contemplation Sutra* states that those who desire birth in that Buddha's Land should "possess the mind of compassion and refrain from killing."[7]

The proscription against taking life was also present in ancient India, prior to the emergence of Buddhism. Jainism, which is said to have arisen at around the same time as Buddhism, also mentions the well-known teaching of the precept not to kill (*ahimsa*). During the Asuka period (ca. seventh century C.E.) in Japan, following the introduction of Buddhism, there was promulgated an official national proclamation—based on this Buddhist teaching—that prohibited the taking of life. It is also known that during the Heian period (ca. ninth to twelfth centuries C.E.), the death penalty was not carried out at all during a 350-year period due to the influence of Buddhist teachings.

The fundamental ethic of Buddhism, then, teaches us to value the lives of all living beings, and cautions us not to take life. However, in today's culture we go about our lives every day consuming fish and meat without giving it a thought. The question we must ask is how we, who are learning the Buddhist teachings, should think about this.

The teaching of Shin Buddhism, which we are now studying, developed as a new path to Buddhahood. Upon that path Shinran was able to realize enlightenment, even though he continued to live the life of a lay householder throughout his life, during which he took part in married life and took the lives of many plants and animals. Within the long history of the transmission of Buddhism, this was the first path formed for the sake of ordinary householders. For that reason, Shin Buddhism has never had any prohibition against eating fish or meat. However, it is still a Buddhist teaching, and so I believe that we should still think carefully about the karmic offense involved in taking life.

I believe that Shinran also ate fish and meat at many times during his life. Among the fragments of writings that he left behind is one entitled "A Passage Concerning Pure Meat." In it he discusses the distinction between pure meat and impure meat, based on the *Mahā Parinirvāṇa Sutra*. He says that Gautama Buddha permitted even renunciant monks to eat meat if the meat was pure, having satisfied certain conditions. We can gather from this that, even though Shinran spent his life as a lay householder and ate fish and meat, he felt a tremendous conflict in his heart regarding the eating of meat, for it was an act committing the karmic offense of taking life. He must have had much concern about this during his life.

Shōma (1800-1872) of Kagawa prefecture was a Shin Buddhist follower who lived in deep *shinjin*. One time he was invited by an acquaintance for a meal of fish and meat, which he had not eaten for some time. It is said that, as he ate the meal, he murmured over and over again, "Taking life is so delicious!" Shōma, it seems, also thought deeply of the contradiction involved in taking life. As he was eating his meal, he must have been apologizing to all of those fish and animals whose lives he was taking. Many of us also eat the meat of fish and other animals in our everyday lives. In today's world, that is a completely natural thing to do. Yet, I believe that, as we carve into our meat, we must also engrave resolutely onto our hearts the Buddhist ethical teaching that we are committing the terrible karmic offense of taking life.

And, I would also like to see that, at the very least, we try carefully to observe the custom of taking at least one vegetarian meal and refraining from eating meat on the day memorializing Shinran's death or the deaths of our own mothers or fathers. This has been a custom in the Shin Buddhist tradition since olden times. In the region of Hiroshima, where I was born and raised, *shinjin* used to flourish long ago, and this custom was faithfully followed in every home. When I was boy, up until the 1940s, approximately 300,000 people lived in the city of Hiroshima. On the sixteenth day of every month, people observed Shinran's memorial day, and every single fish and meat shop in the city of Hiroshima was closed. On that day, no one ate fish or meat. However, since the Second World War and the dropping of the atomic bomb this practice has died out. I find this very regrettable.

The Logic of Harmonious Living

I believe that this Buddhist ethical teaching not to take life is likely to become an important instinction for the world and for humanity from now on. The modern age began from the standpoint of the autonomy of human reason. With it, earlier religious worldviews were discarded, and a new, human-centered viewpoint was established. One result of that was the formation and development of science, which explained everything in the natural world scientifically and rationally, and eventually came to control and gain mastery over it. Traditions of human society as well were rejected, and rational reforms of them were advanced, based on the principle of human self-determination. In this way, human beings gradually created a society of utility, convenience, and comfort. The development of scientific culture has brought about improvements to everyday life, which continue up to the present day.

However, the reverse side of that development is revealed in the current state of the planet and the growing problem of environmental destruction. The phenomenon of global warming has rapidly arisen as the result of our consumption of various forms of energy, and the ice at both polar caps is now melting. The tropical rainforests are being destroyed one after another by unrestricted logging.

The earth's greenery is being reduced, and many places are being rapidly turned into deserts. Also, the burning of plastic and other trash is generating poisonous dioxin. The atmosphere is becoming more and more polluted, and the destruction of the ozone layer is growing progressively worse. Further, the pollution of our water sources is becoming more and more severe in many places around the world, thereby threatening the security of water resources which are used for everyday subsistence, agriculture, and industry. In addition, we have not yet resolved many of the problems pertaining to nuclear generators, such as how we should dispose of their highly dangerous waste products.

We have secured a life of utility and comfort through the development of our modern scientific culture. On the other hand, we are now looking at such impending environmental destruction that even the very existence of the human race is being imperiled. Those of us living today must bear a heavy responsibility for these problems, and we must answer to all of the generations that will come after us.

In addition, numerous conflicts continue to arise throughout the world. They result from disagreements between nations, struggles between peoples, and hostility between religions. This is truly a deplorable situation. In this twenty-first century, how foolish and tragic is this thing we call war. We human beings ought to know well and keenly that we can gain nothing at all and lose so much through war. And yet, in spite of that, wars seem to occur over and over again even today. Without question, we must once again ponder the depth of our human ego-attachment and karmic offenses. I believe, as a follower of the Buddhist teachings, that the precept not to take life, which Gautama Buddha taught to us long ago, is a vital instruction, which is of utmost importance to all of us in the world today, and it must never be forgotten.

It is necessary that we once again engage in a critical and comprehensive re-examination of the way in which human beings have been living in modern times, and reconsider the remnants that we have been leaving behind. How should we live from now on? First of all, I believe that we ought to become critically aware that the human way of looking at things and our modern way of life have been entirely centered on material objects. We have been paying little attention to the spiritual aspects of life. Also, we grasp everything dualistically, viewing the self and others in opposition to each other. Thus, our science has led us to see nature as an object for our use, and so we think only of gaining mastery over and controlling it.

We use Charles Darwin's (1809-1882) theory of evolution to argue that today's advances have come about through our struggles with others and the competition for survival. Marx's *Capital*, for instance, asserts that all structures of society occur within the antagonistic relationship between the capitalist and worker classes, and that societal change and progress will only take place through class struggle. This contention is based on a viewpoint that grasps all structures of this world in terms of the opposition and conflict between the self and other. Yet, is that the true nature of the world of living beings or of human society? I believe that it is necessary for us to ponder this again very carefully.

From the perspective of the Buddhist teaching, all things that live on this earth are interconnected within life. Furthermore, in its Chinese and Japanese developments, Buddhism says that that we share a basic commonality of life with all plants and trees, and also all land and minerals. According to this conception, each existence on this earth is connected to all other things—in conditional arising, all are respectively equal and their existences have meaning, for they all depend on each other and assist one another. It follows that we should not divide off the self from others, nor think of them as being in opposition or in struggle with each other. Instead, we need to recognize each other mutually and reciprocally, and see that self and others live in non-dualistic harmony.

Hence, I believe the ideas of not taking life and of harmonious living, both of which recognize the basic commonality of all life, serve as the starting points for Buddhist ethics. As such, even more attention must be paid to them in the coming years. From that start, we will be able to embark on a way of living through which we will discover at the root of all existence the significance of this life—each unique, personal life—and we will be able to awaken to its dignity, pour out our love and affection to it, and try to nurture it. And, inevitably, each of us will come to wish for peace in the world as we reflect upon ways in which we are conducting our lives. As we seek to bring our own wasteful desires under control, it is likely that we will come to live lives of "lessening desires and realizing fulfillment" as taught in the *Mahā Parinirvāṇa Sutra*.

In order for the twenty-first century to become a period of brilliance during which today's global crises, conflicts, and strife are overcome, there can be nothing more vital than for us to establish a new human way of life. We must fundamentally alter the way in which we think about the structure of the existence of human beings and the world. We must change from the materialistic viewpoint of the past to a perspective centered on spirituality and on our hearts and minds. We must discard our attachment to dualistic opposition and adopt an approach that values non-dualistic harmony and the basic commonality of all life. I think that, in order for that to happen, the instructions not to take life and to live in harmony, which Eastern thought and Buddhist ethics teach, will bear much importance.

A True Disciple of the Buddha

Soft and Gentle Heart—Firm and Resolute Mind

Shinran says that one who lives in *shinjin* is a "true disciple of the Buddha." Here, "disciple of the Buddha" means a disciple of Gautama Buddha. That is to say, when we say the *nembutsu* and realize *shinjin*—the experience of awakening—we become Gautama's true disciples. Gautama Buddha may have lived in the distant past. But, Shinran says, we who live in *shinjin* here and now immediately cross over that long span of time and join the assembly gathering to hear Gautama Buddha's exposition of the dharma. Hence, we become genuine disciples of the Buddha and true Buddhist followers.

Shinran then explains that a true disciple of the Buddha is endowed in mind and body with two kinds of benefit, and cites passages from the Thirty-third and Thirty-fourth Vows from the forty-eight Vows of Amida Buddha, which are expounded in the *Larger Sutra of Immeasurable Life*. The Thirty-third Vow declares that, "upon being touched by the light, one becomes soft and gentle." This means that when we have attained true and real *shinjin*, and have come to know dharma-truth and been touched by the light of Amida Buddha, we will realize a benefit whereby we become soft and gentle in body and mind. No matter what events may take place in the lives of those who live in the *nembutsu* and *shinjin*, our hearts and bodies will always be soft and gentle. Instead of trying to avoid another person or deny a situation, we will be able to open our hearts widely to accept that person or admit to those circumstances.

However, to become soft and gentle in heart and mind does not mean that we become mushy or weak-willed. On the contrary, it means that we resolutely establish our own personal subjectivity, and possess minds of a firmness that cannot be destroyed by anything at all. Thus, Shinran also refers to *shinjin* as the "diamond-like mind" because a diamond is the hardest of all things. Furthermore, because our minds are firm and resolute, our hearts can be soft, gentle, and accepting of anything at all. Therefore, he also understands *shinjin* to be the "soft and gentle mind," for it can be the softest and gentlest of all things.

Hence, in Shin Buddhism *shinjin* means that we live with hearts and minds that are hard and yet soft, gentle and yet resolute. This is the fundamental image of the lives of those who live in *shinjin*. Because our minds are firm and resolute, we will never lose sight of our selves no matter what situation we are facing. And we will always be able to establish and firmly maintain our own personal subjectivity. There may be times when we find ourselves going against the currents of society. We may experience isolation and come face-to-face with severe challenges, without any help. Yet, to live in *shinjin* means that, even if that should be so, we would never allow ourselves to give in to the oncoming stream, but would instead stand straightly, and independently, within it.

And yet, at the same time, living in *shinjin* also means that we are soft and gentle in heart and body. Buddhism teaches that to be of the same essence with another is literally to be of the "same body" with that person. When we abandon our own egos and view things from the perspective of another, then we become of the same body as that person. We are able to take in our fellow beings within our soft and gentle hearts, and then exert all of our efforts for their sakes. Those who live in *shinjin* must not forget to live with minds that are firm and resolute and hearts that are soft and gentle. This is the heart-mind that allows us to be of the "same body" with others.

According to the life stories of Shinran, a person of different religious persuasion had long hated him. The man hatched a scheme to kill Shinran and broke into his home with that intention. Shinran somehow knew of the plan, however, and, even when attacked by the man, did not become angry at him. Instead, he received the man into his home with a gentle smile on his face. This affected the man greatly, and his heart was moved by the warmth of Shinran's personality. As a result, the man expressed remorse for his evil thoughts and became one of Shinran's followers. This episode illustrates for us Shinran's soft and gentle heart.

At the same time, Shinran was also consistently critical of those who failed to understand the Buddha-dharma correctly and committed evil acts as a result. Once, he instructed his followers that none should associate closely with such persons. He also warned that such persons would not be allowed to sit in the same dharma halls with others. This is an example of the more severe and stern aspects of Shinran's firm and resolute mind. Living in *shinjin* means that one must live with a heart that is soft and yet hard, and a mind that is firm and yet gentle.

Eyes that See Beyond the Secular World

Next, the Thirty-fourth Vow states that, "upon hearing the Name, one will attain insight into the non-origination of all existences." Upon saying the *nembutsu* and hearing the Buddha's calling voice, we realize true and real *shinjin* and attain a benefit. The benefit is that we are able to gain insight into the non-origination of all things, which is true wisdom.

Attaining wisdom means that we come to possess eyes through which we are able to perceive this secular world critically, with wisdom that transcends the world. We are able to thoroughly de-absolutize all of the value systems of this secular world, and critically observe all of their various states from a point of view that sees beyond the secular world, even while we live in the midst of this world. In other words, we are able to observe society from a critical perspective—with eyes that are able to perceive correctly through all of the distorted images and contradictions created by society, and into the falsity and empty truths that lie concealed within this secular world.

Because such distortions and falsity originate out of the ego-attachment and ego-desire of human beings, they have existed and will continue to exist in all times and at all places, within every sort of power structure, social order, and political and economic system in every society in this world. Yet, one who is truly living in *shinjin* is able to see the reality of such distortions and falsity. This leads to unrelenting criticism of the contradictions, oppression, and discrimination that exist in society, and then to action intended to resolve them. This, fundamentally, is the image of a human being who lives in *shinjin*.

In the past, however, the idea of *shinjin* in Shin Buddhism was not considered to be so dynamic or active. The reason is that the Shin Buddhist teachings were interpreted in ways that would make followers simply submit to the prevailing power structures of the day and obediently adhere to that social order. As a result, eyes that might criticize and de-absolutize the worldly value systems

—eyes that *shinjin* ought to have—were not nurtured at all. Today, we must try to learn the Shin Buddhist teachings correctly and establish true *shinjin* as we critically scrutinize past doctrinal understandings.

Based on his own *shinjin*, Shinran severely criticized the actual state of the Buddhist and religious worlds of his time, and classified them into three types: (1) true teachings, (2) provisional teachings, and (3) false teachings. Shinran rejected all teachings other than Buddhism, calling them all false teachings. He also criticized the Buddhist teachings that prospered by adhering themselves to the ruling authorities, saying that they were all provisional or expedient teachings that were presented in order to guide persons eventually to the truth. Finally, he took the position that Shin Buddhism—the teaching of the *nembutsu* of the Primal Vow—alone was the true and real teaching.

In addition, Shinran clearly criticized the political authorities of his day for acting contrary to the truth. He referred to those in power and the people who were following after them as "outsiders." One should not, he said, join hands with such persons or think about spreading the dharma to them. For saying this, Shinran was denounced by many persons of his time. Yet, I feel that, through the clear wisdom of his *shinjin*—his eyes that were able to see beyond this world—Shinran was able to see through the distortions and falsity that filled the world. And he saw

Shin Buddhist Life

with those eyes throughout his entire life, as we can tell from these words from *A Record in Lament of Divergences*:

> But with a foolish being full of blind passions, in this fleeting world—this burning house—all matters without exception are empty and false, totally without truth and sincerity. The nembutsu alone is true and real.[8]

I would like all of us also to learn of the true *shinjin* of Shin Buddhism, and live with eyes of firm and resolute wisdom, so that we may be able to de-absolutize and criticize this secular world.

A Single, Unhindered Path

Shinran also says that a "single, unhindered path" will open up, without fail, within the life of the person of true *nembutsu* and *shinjin*. It will be a path of peace and tranquility, which will be unhindered by any difficulty or obstruction.

As we have seen earlier, living in the *shinjin* of Shin Buddhism means that we will live with a heart and mind and body that are soft and gentle. Our hearts will be soft and yet hard, firm and yet gentle. It also means that we will be able to attain wisdom and, with eyes that see beyond this world, will be able to critically perceive the distortions and falsity of actual society and thereupon act courageously to resolve them. In *shinjin* we will inevitably be endowed with such benefits. However, in reality our lives are not that way at all, for we are constantly hindered by many internal, unseen obstructions and many external, visible obstructions.

Shan-tao of China offered an illustration of a life of *nembutsu* and *shinjin*. In it he says that human life is like walking on a single white path that lies between a river of surging water and a river of raging fire. The river of water represents our hearts of desire, while the river of fire symbolizes our minds of wrath. The white path that lies between the two rivers refers to our lives of *nembutsu* and *shinjin*. The width of that path, he says, is only four to five *sun*. In Shan-tao's China one *sun* was equivalent to the width of one human finger. Thus, a path of four or five *sun* is approximately the width of a person's hand—truly a narrow and perilous path. The water and fire, moreover, are constantly descending upon the path in furious waves. This reflects the actual state of our human lives of *nembutsu* and *shinjin*. Why would Shan-tao say that the path of *shinjin* is such a narrow path? This teaching forces us to think deeply upon ourselves.

As we do, we realize that our progress along the path is

Shin Buddhist Life

constantly being obstructed by our foolish minds of self-attachment—our hearts that are endlessly craving the objects of our desire (river of water) and our minds that are always driving away things that we detest (river of fire). On occasion, they may even cause us to fall disastrously into the rivers of water and fire. Shan-tao explains that many bandits and evil beasts—terrifying people and animals—call out loudly to us from behind as we walk on this white path, warning us that the path is very dangerous and urging us to come back.

I believe that, in Shan-tao's parable, the rivers of fire and water represent our internal, unseen obstructions that block the path of *nembutsu* and *shinjin*, while the voices calling out from the rear refer to external and visible obstructions.

As we seek to live in *nembutsu* and *shinjin*, we are constantly being impeded by the defiled passions of our foolish selves, our minds of ego-attachment and self-desire, which think only of what is good for us, and our hearts of greed and wrath. We thus cause ourselves endless troubles. In other words, there is a battle going on within ourselves. It is conflict between our selves, who are being nurtured by the Buddha, and our selves, who are lumps of ego-attachment and ego-desire, unchanged since we were born. These internal obstructions are represented in this parable by the rivers of fire and water.

Our external obstructions are also represented by the many bandits and evil beasts who are calling out to us from behind to return from the path. Concretely speaking, these refer to all of the many worldly values, which are the objects of our numerous desires, such as love, wealth, or fame. Such values often appear and disappear before our very eyes, always pulling at our legs from behind. As long as we live in this world, these worldly values will assume various guises as they approach us, and seek to tempt us with their charms. They constantly press in upon us and they are charged with danger, for they risk becoming massive obstructions that will block our way, or make us plummet into the rivers of fire and water. This is the battle that continues to rage within, between, and around our selves.

However, Shinran explains that one who lives the true path of *nembutsu* and *shinjin* is able to cross directly over the rivers of peril on that white path of human life—a single, unhindered path—no matter how narrow or full of obstructions that path may be. For those of us who are learning of the *nembutsu* and *shinjin* of Shin Buddhism, this is a message that ought to be deeply considered and truly appreciated.

Chapter Three

The Shin Buddhist Way of Life

Living with "Prayers for the World"

Shinran's Instruction

We will continue to address the question of how *shinjin* relates to society by taking a closer look at the way in which we can live as Shin Buddhist followers. Let us begin by examining Shinran's instructions to his followers that they should "live with prayers for the world." In a letter to them he states,

I hope that everyone will, deeply entrusting

themselves to the nembutsu and firmly embracing prayers [for the world] in their hearts, together say the nembutsu.⁹

The phrase "prayers for the world" precedes a passage in the same letter that states,

Those who feel that their own birth is completely settled should, mindful of the Buddha's benevolence, hold the nembutsu in their hearts and say it to respond in gratitude to that benevolence with the wish, "May there be peace in the world and may the Buddha's teaching spread!"¹⁰

Shinran's words urge all of us to engage in heartfelt prayers or aspirations for peace in today's society and for the flourishing of the Buddha-dharma.

Here the word "prayer" is a translation of the Japanese word *inoru*. The first portion of the word, *i*, has the meaning of "reverence, discretion, or restraint." The second portion, *noru*, means "to tell, inform, proclaim, or signify." Thus, inoru means that one reverently proclaims one's heartfelt aspiration before the gods and Buddhas, and acts to bring about the fulfillment of that wish. Here, I believe that Shinran's words, "prayers for the world," signify his proclamation to the Buddha of his own aspirations for the state of the world and society, and also the actions that he had undertaken to actualize his prayers.

What, then, would be the content of the prayer that we might proclaim to the Buddha? Shinran, unfortunately, does not provide us with any specific details. However, I believe that our prayer must contain our aspiration to live our lives, learn the Buddha-dharma, and direct ourselves to the Pure Land. And, it will be fulfilled when we take Amida Buddha's Vow above all else as our own vow, and make Amida's wish our own wish. Therefore, "prayers for the world" require that we learn of Amida Buddha's Primal Vow—the Buddha's wish for us, which is revealed in the forty-eight Vows.

Amida Buddha's Vows

Amida Buddha made forty-eight Vows. The content of those Vows can be arranged into four categories.
1. **First through Eleventh Vows.**
These comprise Vows for the adornments of the Buddha's Land. Amida Buddha has selected and designed these Vows to establish a Buddha-land of freedom and equality—a Pure Land—as the ideal world, which the realm of humans might someday become.
2. **Twelfth through Seventeenth Vows.**
These are Vows for the adornments of the Buddha's body.

These Vows are designed so that, upon realizing enlightenment, Amida will become a Buddha possessed of this kind of character. Also, he vows that, as a Buddha, he will take the name "Namu Amida Butsu" and draw near to all beings as that calling voice.

3. **Eighteenth, Nineteenth, and Twentieth Vows.**

These are Amida Buddha's Vows to take in and hold sentient beings. These Vows are designed to be the methods for our salvation. The first of these Vows sets out the true path for attaining Buddhahood through the *nembutsu*. This is the path of the Eighteenth Vow, which entails the authentic experience of awakening or *shinjin*. The latter two Vows then disclose two expedient paths or processes. The path of the Nineteenth Vow is the *nembutsu* path of sundry practices and mixed praxis. This path mixes together many different practices for the sake of those whose understanding of the path of enlightenment is still insufficient. The path of the Twentieth Vow is the *nembutsu* path of the exclusive practice of the *nembutsu*.

However, no one achieves the experience of awakening on these paths. Instead, the path of sundry practices and mixed praxis (Nineteenth Vow) and the path of the exclusive practice of the *nembutsu* (Twentieth Vow) both serve as provisional teachings or expedient means. In them, Amida Buddha aspires to draw in and nurture all people equally so that we may realize the true path of attaining enlightenment through the *nembutsu*, which entails *shinjin*, or the experience of awakening of the Eighteenth Vow.

4. **Twenty-first through Forty-eighth Vows.**

These remaining Vows set forth the benefits of salvation, which are experienced by those who live in the true *nembutsu*. The Vows reveal not only benefits that are realized in this present life, but also benefits to be realized after death, in the life to come. Shinran gave special attention to the Twenty-second Vow of "directing virtue in the aspect of returning to this world," which is one of the benefits to be attained in the world after death.

I believe that the Vows of Amida Buddha that correspond to Shinran's "prayers for the world" are the First through the Eleventh Vows—the Vows for the adornment of the Buddha's land. These represent eleven kinds of aspiration or wishes through which the Buddha sought to establish the Pure Land as the ideal world for human beings.

Vows for the Adornment of the Buddha's Land

All eleven Vows for the adornment of the Buddha's Land are encapsulated in the first four Vows.

The First Vow. Here the Buddha vows that in the Buddha's Land, the three evil realms of hell, hungry ghosts, and animals will be non-existent. In other words, it represents the wish that the three kinds of defiled passions, which are greed, anger, and foolishness, will not exist within us.

The Second Vow. This is the Vow that beings in that land will not fall back into evil realms, so that no one will return to the place from which they came. This indicates the Buddha's wish that even though our defiled passions may have been extinguished just a little, still we will not revert once again to the way we originally were.

Therefore, in the First and Second Vows Amida Buddha aspires for the ideal state of being of humanness for each one of us.

The Third Vow. Here Amida vows that all beings in that land will be the color of gold. This represents the wish that when we realize birth in the Pure Land, we will all become persons who shine brilliantly like the color of gold.

The Fourth Vow. This is the Vow that no one will have any likes or dislikes. This represents the Buddha's wish that all beings will be wholesome and unbiased in body and mind, and that there will be no discrimination between beauty and ugliness, or high and low. All will be equal.

Therefore, in the Third and Fourth Vows Amida Buddha aspires for the ideal state of human society.

In this way, the first four Vows declare the fundamental principles that form the ideals for human beings and our world. They elucidate the wish that we human beings may, first of all, cast off our old selves and realize true growth within ourselves so that we may become, even little by little, the ideal human beings that we ought to be. And, they also set forth the aspiration that our human world may overcome all discrimination and conflict, and grow into full maturity as an ideal society of harmony and equality, which it ought to be. Thus, the first four Vows of Amida Buddha set forth the images of an ideal world and ideal humanity.

The Fifth through Tenth Vows describe the content of the first four Vows in greater detail.

The Fifth Vow—that beings in the Buddha's land will thoroughly remember all past lives. As ideal beings, we will possess the ability to perceive the very origins and roots of our lives.

The Sixth Vow—that beings in that land will know thoroughly with divine eyes. We will possess the ability to perceive the real state of the world, which exists as a result of mutual dependence and mutual support.

The Seventh Vow—that beings in that land will know thoroughly with divine ears. We will possess the ability to hear with ears of the mind, so that we can perceive the voices of joy and sadness of all living beings in the world.

The Eighth Vow—that beings in that land will know thoroughly the hearts and minds of others. We will possess the ability to understand deeply the thoughts and feelings of all people in the world. That is, we will empathize with them and suffer in the same way that they suffer.

The Ninth Vow—that beings in that land will be able to know thoroughly by using their supernatural legs to travel in an instant to any distant place, wherever it may be. We will possess the ability to go to the side of those who are suffering or in anguish. We will also be able to think and act from the standpoint of any individual.

The Tenth Vow—that beings of that land will know thoroughly by extinguishing all passions. We will have the ability to transform and overcome all of the defiled passions that we human beings possess, that is, all of the workings of our minds of self-attachment.

These six Vows all contain the Buddha's wish that beings living in the ideal world will possess the six kinds of abilities that transcend this secular world. These are referred to as the "six transcendent abilities." Certainly, if the world were inhabited only by beings having the ability to know, perceive, or act in this way, then it would be a place of true peace and happiness, devoid of any sorts of conflict or strife.

The Eleventh Vow—that beings in that land will necessarily attain nirvana. The preceding Sixth through Tenth Vows all merge within this Vow, for it reveals that the ultimate perfection of those Vows is the enlightenment of the Buddha and the establishment of that Buddha's realm of the Pure Land, which are the ultimate goals that the Buddhist teachings direct us to attain.

The Vows indeed reveal that the realm of Amida Buddha—the Pure Land—is to be recognized as the ideal world, which our own human society can become. Many people today grasp the Pure Land abstractly, simply as a world that exists after death. However, that is not a correct understanding. Understood properly, the Pure Land is the ultimate and ideal realm, which this earth and today's human society should constantly aim to become. In that sense, I believe that we should strive as one to make this planet reflect, even just a little, that Pure Land of the Buddha. This is particularly important today, when conflicts and disputes arise throughout the globe and the destruction of the environment is growing so horrific that the very life of our planet is exposed to grave danger. We may even say that the attempt to make this world a reflection of the Pure Land is the most pressing task facing humanity today. Shinran teaches us this way to live as human beings when he instructs us to think, "May the world be at peace!" and urges us to live with "prayers for the world."

The Wish for Human Fulfillment

True Freedom

We have seen that the First and Second of Amida

Buddha's Vows express the ideal state of human-ness that each individual may become. In Buddhist terms, here the Buddha aspires that each and every being will realize true awakening and become a Buddha. Some of the expressions used to describe the Buddha include "free person" or "one who is emancipated." Thus, it is the Buddha's wish that all will become truly "free persons" or "emancipated beings."

The origin of the modern Japanese words *jiyū* (freedom) and *jizai* (liberty) can be found in ancient Chinese texts. Both words have long been mentioned in Buddhist literature as well. When employed as technical Buddhist terms, *jiyū* and *jizai* signify that one is able to overcome both one's defiled passions and the working of one's self-centered mind. Hence, one is able to achieve personal transformation and become an ideal human being. This is the Buddhist sense of the words *jiyū* and *jizai*, which, as we can see, differs completely from the modern sense of freedom and liberty. That is, today the words imply that one becomes free from some kind of restriction and is able to conduct oneself as one pleases or sees fit. In that case, freedom would be "freedom from something."

However, in Buddhism, freedom is "freedom to become something." Buddhism directs us toward our true growth as human beings. As I mentioned in the very first chapter, this means that we live according to universal principles, while at the same time we shoulder responsibility for our own lives. When we come to live at the intersection of those vertical and horizontal axes, at that very moment, we are able to establish our true personal and individual subjectivity. We are able to live in genuine reliance upon ourselves and live as we are, unharmed by anything that may surround us.

Ordinarily, we do not live with this kind of independence. Usually, we worry about how other people view us and allow ourselves to be dependent on something or someone else. However, when we realize true enlightenment and establish our true selves, then we will be able to live in reliance upon ourselves and exist as we are. This is the reason why the Buddha is called a "free person" and "one who is emancipated."

The Process of Human Fulfillment

When we live with "prayers for the world," here and now, the wishes that Amida Buddha makes for us, as expressed in the First and Second Vows, become our own wishes as well. For each of us, our ideal state of being becomes manifest in an ongoing process of human fulfillment, which continues throughout our lives. As we constantly learn the Buddha-dharma and say the *nembutsu*, we continue to awaken to our being "free persons" and "emancipated beings" in our lives of *shinjin*. This kind of personal transformation or human fulfillment takes place only within true and real *shinjin*.

Shinran, moreover, describes this idea of true growth as a human being when he called the person of *shinjin* a "bodhisattva,"[11] one who "will attain Buddhahood,"[12] and "a person who is equal to the Tathagatas."[13] Shinran understood that as long as we humans live in this secular world, it will be impossible for us to attain Buddhahood. Therefore, he did not refer to a person who is living in deep *shinjin* as a "Buddha" or "Tathagata." Instead, he used the expressions "a person who will eventually become a Buddha" or said that although such a person is not a Tathagata, such a person is "equal to the Tathagatas."

This does not imply that in *shinjin* the path to enlightenment is not yet complete. Rather, living in *shinjin* means that "in the preceding moment, life ends....[I]n the next moment, [we] are immediately born."[14] When we reject and abandon our lives of delusion, we are able to live by receiving the life of the Buddha. Hence, it may be said that the entirety of the Buddhist path is brought to completion in *shinjin*. Beyond that, nothing need be added. *Shinjin* alone is sufficient.

And yet, although everything has been brought to perfection in *shinjin*, we still have physical bodies and thus will retain many defiled passions throughout our lives. And, as long as we do, we continue to live lives bound for hell.

Shin Buddhist Life

We possess hellish lives, and yet also, we are enabled to live —here and now—because we have received the life of the Buddha. This is the true reality of living in the *shinjin* of Shin Buddhism. For this reason Shinran does not directly refer to the person of *shinjin* as a Buddha, but rather as "one who will attain Buddhahood" or "a person equal to the Tathagatas." All the more so, then, we must continue to engage in the process of human fulfillment by cherishing the *nembutsu* and deepening our *shinjin* on this path of becoming Buddhas.

Aspiring for the Fulfillment of Society

True Equality

We have also seen that in the Third and Fourth Vows, Amida Buddha aspires for the ideal state of humanity and the world. If we were to express this in Buddhist terms, it would mean that the Buddha wishes for a realm of humanity that will mature into a world that is truly equal and without discrimination.

Here as well, the origins of the modern Japanese word *byōdō* (equality) can be seen in many Buddhist texts. As generally understood today, *byōdō* has such meanings as "mutually equivalent," "of the same rank," or that "all are uniform and the same." However, in the Buddhist sense of equality all existence is comprehended not simply from a secular viewpoint, but also from the standpoint of non-self (*anatman*), which negates the ego-self. The latter perceives the existence of every thing in terms of its own individual nature, and yet also perceives all things equally and without discrimination, as existences supported and enveloped by truth. Therefore, equality in the Buddhist teachings means that all relationships of conflict between rulers and the ruled, or oppressors and the oppressed, are eliminated. Each thing possesses its own individuality and dignity, and stands independently in the significance of its existence. And yet, at the same time, all things are in harmony with one another and coexist within an entire whole. The establishment of that totality gives rise to the ideal world, and this is the meaning of equality in Buddhism.

The Process of Societal Fulfillment

When we follow Shinran's instruction to live with "prayers for the world," our wishes for the state of today's society coincide with Amida Buddha's wishes, which are expressed in the Third and Fourth Vows. Here, the ideal state of our world takes the form of an ongoing process of societal fulfillment. Each and every day of our lives of *shinjin* we say the *nembutsu* and direct our actions toward the fulfillment of a society of true equality. This kind of

Shin Buddhist Life

societal reformation or fulfillment takes place only when we live in true and real *shinjin*.

As we have seen above, the wish expressed in the Third Vow is that all beings in the Pure Land will shine brilliantly like the color of gold. The aspiration of the Fourth Vow is that all beings in the Pure Land will be wholesome and unbiased in body and mind, and that there will be no discrimination between beauty and ugliness, or high and low. That is, all will be viewed with equality.

These Vows allow us to speculate as to the background out of which the *Larger Sutra of Immeasurable Life* arose. It is likely that in feudal societies of ancient northwestern India, there existed terrible discrimination among peoples and races on the basis of the color of their skin. It is also likely that many kinds of discrimination existed in that social system, between the noble and humble, the rich and poor. We can surmise that the Vows of this sutra were written so as to issue a scathing criticism of the conditions that existed in society of that time.

Gautama Buddha fundamentally rejected all such societal discrimination and taught of the state of true equality. This sutra passage clearly expresses his teaching:

> Not by birth is one an outcast; not by birth is one a brahman. By deed one becomes an outcast, by deed one becomes a brahman.[15]

A society of equality, where no discrimination exists, is the true state of society and the ideal image of the human realm. However, "equality" does not require that everyone be the same, standing uniformly in single file. Rather, each and every being exists in his or her own individuality and dignity, and each individual is enabled to live within the full significance of her or his own existence. And, at the same time, all beings coexist in a harmony of the whole. This is the meaning of an ideal world of equality.

The process of bringing about the fulfillment of a society of equality involves our continuous efforts to bring about even a slight reflection of the image of the Pure Land within the current state of today's world. Further, it will involve our efforts to create a world in which individual benefits can be obtained only when everyone is able to benefit together. This process, I believe, is none other than to live the path of the bodhisattva—a path in which self and other are one—the basic spirit of which is found in the bodhisattva's vow: "As long as all living beings have not yet attained enlightenment, I will also not attain Buddhahood."

As I reflect upon this, I have come to believe strongly that Miyazawa Kenji (1896–1933), a writer of Japanese children's literature, truly lived the path of a bodhisattva, for he possessed prayers for human fulfillment and prayers for societal fulfillment. He was born in Iwate prefecture during the Meiji period to parents who were devout Shin

Shin Buddhist Life 231

Buddhist followers. By the time Miyazawa was three years old he could recite Shinran's entire "Hymn of True Shinjin and the Nembutsu" (Shōshinge) from memory. As a middle school student he was deeply fascinated by *A Record in Lament of Divergences*. Finally, he came to read the *Lotus Sutra* and was strongly drawn to the Mahayana Buddhist idea of the oneness of self and other. This Mahayana Buddhist principle finds passionate expression in many of his literary works. Here is an example:

> If the entire world is not happy, then there can be no individual happiness. Our consciousness of the self must expand gradually from the individual to the group, and then to society and the universe. Is this not the kind of path that ancient sages also treaded and spoke of? In this new age, the world is becoming a single consciousness; it is seeking to become a living organism. We are able to live with truth and vitality when we become aware of the existence of the universe within ourselves, and seek to live in accordance with it. May we always search for true happiness in the world, for searching is our path.[16]

This passage was written by a person who clearly understood, and lived, the principles of Buddhism. As we learn Shinran's teachings of Shin Buddhism and live on the path of the *nembutsu* we would do well to reflect on the path of Miyazawa Kenji and to embrace his aspiration.

Of course, this may just be a dream, when we consider the actual state of today's world. However, I believe that it is a magnificent dream—one that we should embrace and establish as our own vow. We can, and should, determine our own way of life as sincere seekers, filled with idealism and free of boundaries. This is the true way of life—living with prayers for the world—of Shin Buddhist followers, who are directed toward the Pure Land.

Directing Virtue in Our Return to This World

Meaning of Birth in the Pure Land

Now we have seen what it means to live in *shinjin*. As individual *nembutsu* followers, we strive for human fulfillment, which means that we direct ourselves toward the attainment of enlightenment, casting off the skin of our old selves and realizing the growth of our new selves. As members of society, we strive to live as bodhisattvas of *shinjin* on the path of self-benefit and benefiting others, realizing that we will find no happiness unless the whole world has realized true happiness.

The bodhisattva path, however, is very difficult to follow, and there are limits to our ability to bring about our own human fulfillment. In real life, limitations exist even within the structure of *shinjin*. And ironically, the more we cast off our old selves and grow into the new, the more aware we become of those limitations. We come to see with stark clarity the old selves that we have not yet cast off, as well as the new selves that we have not yet grown into. The more we are illuminated by the light of the Pure Land, the more the shadow of our own personal hell becomes visible to our eyes. Thus, although Shinran says that the path of enlightenment is brought to completion in *shinjin*, he does not say that a person of *shinjin* has become a Buddha. Instead, he explains that we attain enlightenment for the first time when we realize birth in the Pure Land after death.

It may even seem that birth in the Pure Land is no longer necessary for those who have already realized *shinjin*, since the path to Buddhahood has already been brought to completion and its ultimate aim has been achieved. And in fact, persons of *shinjin* need no longer wonder about whether or not they will be born in the Pure Land after death. Why, then, did Shinran take up the question of birth in the Pure Land after death? I believe that it was not for the sake of persons of *shinjin*. Rather, the purpose for birth in the Pure Land is solely to bring about the salvation and enlightenment of all other beings.

As we have already seen, any social activism that is

based in *shinjin*—the activity of benefiting others with the mind that saves beings—will involve acts undertaken in the midst of this present world. Naturally, then, it will be limited in many different ways. Thus, Shinran says,

> Compassion in the Pure Land Path should be understood as first attaining Buddhahood quickly through saying the nembutsu and, with the mind of great love and great compassion, freely benefiting sentient beings as one wishes.[17]

When we attain birth in the Pure Land and realize enlightenment, then for the first time we will be able to benefit and save beings, just as we would like. Here Shinran declares that after we have been born in the Pure Land following our deaths and we become true Buddhas, then we will take part in Amida Buddha's movement to save sentient beings. It is then that we will truly be able to save beings. In Shinran's writings, this activity is called "directing of virtue in the aspect of our return to this world" (*gensō ekō*).

As established by Amida Buddha's Vow, "directing of virtue in the aspect of our return to this world" is a benefit that is realized by those who have attained birth in the Pure Land after death. "Aspect of our return" points to our return from the Pure Land to the reality of this present world. "Directing virtue" refers to Amida Buddha's activity that directs itself toward beings. When we become truly enlightened (true Buddhas) in the Pure Land, we are able to participate in this activity of Amida Buddha. Hence, we come back immediately to this world and are able to work actively to save other beings. One who goes to the Pure Land immediately returns to this world. Accordingly, it is said, the Pure Land is devoid of people, for no one remains there.

After death, therefore, we begin to engage in a new movement to bring other beings to Buddhahood. There will be limitations to any activity that we may undertake for others in today's world. Hence in a sense, we take up this aspiration after we die, and join in the movement of Amida Buddha's great love and compassion, thereby acting to bring happiness to all persons and to enable all beings to attain Buddhahood. This notion of "directing of virtue in the aspect of our return to this world" represents a unique feature of Pure Land Buddhist logic and the teaching of Amida Buddha, which is rooted completely in the Mahayana principle of the oneness of self and other.

Persons who Direct Virtue in Their Return to This World

It follows that the most important thing to do as we learn the Buddhist path of enlightenment is to meet our forebears in *shinjin* and the *nembutsu*—persons who have come back from the Pure Land for our sake, and are directing virtue in the aspect of their return to this world. Of course, because our eyes are covered with defiled passions, we are not able to know for certain who such persons may be. As a result, it is unlikely that we will have any direct encounter with persons who are directing virtue in their return to this world. Yet, if we seriously seek the path of Buddhahood, we will inevitably be nurtured by such persons.

Certainly, we will be able to meet persons who are now living in the *nembutsu* and *shinjin* in this life. And when we do, we will also come to perceive, albeit faintly, moving ahead of such living persons, a current of great love and compassion that is coming from the Pure Land. That activity, I believe, will be none other than that of directing of virtue by persons in the aspect of their return to this world, as they take in and guide us to the truth. In sum, in order for us to realize *shinjin*, it is most essential that we encounter the activity of persons who have come from the Pure Land, through the personalities of our living forebears in *shinjin* who have been nurtured by them.

Learning the Buddha-dharma and seeking the path of Buddhahood requires first of all that we meet persons who have come to live in *shinjin* and the *nembutsu* before us. If we do not meet such persons and encounter their lives, then we will never be able to meet the Buddha. If, on the other hand, we are able to encounter such good friends and teachers, then, I believe, we will truly be able to encounter the Buddha. Shinran's own path, which he has left for us, will also continue to teach and guide us. It is my hope that we will all devote our lives to searching for such good teachers of the Way.

NOTES

1 Rennyo, *Goichidaiki Kikigaki* (*The Words of the Master Rennyo, heard and recorded throughout his life*), in Jōdo Shinshū Hongwanji-ha, *Jōdo Shinshū Seiten*: chushakuban, hereinafter JSS (Kyoto: Hongwanji Shuppan-bu, 1988), 1284.
2 See Rennyo, *Letters of Rennyo* (*Gobunshō*), V: 10, JSS, pp. 1196–1997, and III: 12, in JSS, 1157.
3 *True Teaching, Practice, and Realization*, in CWS, 289.
4 *Notes on 'Essentials of Faith Alone,'* in CWS, 453.
5 *Hymns of the Pure Land Masters*, # 40, in CWS, 371.
6 *Sutta-nipāta, Kūlavagga, Dhammika sutta*, 19, trans. John D. Ireland (Kandy: Buddhist Publication Society, 1999)
7 Ryūkoku University Translation Center, *The Sutra of Contemplation on the Buddha of Immeasurable Life* (Kyoto: Ryūkoku University, 1984), 23.
8 *A Record in Lament of Divergences*, Postscript, in CWS, 679.
9 *A Collection of Letters* (*Goshōsokushū*), 2, in CWS, 560 Words in brackets added.

10 Ibid.
11 *Gutoku's Notes* (*Gutokushō*), in CWS, 594.
12 The Virtue of the Name of Amida Tathagata (*Mida nyorai myōgotōku*), in CWS, 657.
13 *Lamp for the Latter Ages* (*Mattōshō*), in CWS, 528.
14 *Gutoku's Notes, in* CWS, 594.
15 *Sutta-nipāta, Uragavagga, Vasala Sutta*, 21, trans. Piyadassi Thera (Kandy: Buddhist Publication Society, 1999)
16 Miyazawa Kenji, "*Nōmin geijutsu gairon kōyō*" ("A Summary and Introduction to the Arts of the Peasantry"), in Takamura Kotaro, ed., Takamura Kotaro, Hagiwara Sakutaro, Miyazawa Kenji shū (Tokyo: Chikuma Shobo, 1954).
17 *A Record in Lament of Divergences*, 4, in CWS, 663.